MALAYSIAN NATURE HANDBOOKS

General Editor

M. W. F. TWEEDIE

THE aim of the Malaysian Nature Handbooks is to provide a series of handy, well-illustrated guides to the fauna and flora of Malaysia and Singapore. They can, of course, be no more than introductory; the animal and plant life of Malaysia is on such a lavish scale that comprehensive accounts of the groups described in each of the Handbooks must be either severely technical or voluminous and correspondingly costly. The selection of species described in each one has been carefully made, however, to illustrate those most likely to be the first encountered by reasonably observant people residing in or visiting Malaysia and Singapore; reference to rarities or species confined to inaccessible country has been avoided, except where such species are of special interest.

It is the Editor's belief that interest in animals and plants is best aroused by providing the means of identifying and naming them. The emphasis of the Handbooks is therefore firstly on identification, but as much information on habits and biology is included as space will allow. It is hoped that they may be of use to schools in supplementing courses in nature study and biology, and a source of pleasure to that quite numerous assemblage of people whose complaint has been that they would gladly be naturalists if someone would show them the way.

MALAYSIAN NATURE HANDBOOKS

Common Malaysian Fruits

BETTY MOLESWORTH ALLEN

Cempedak di luar pagar,
Ambil galah tolong jolokkan:
Sahaya budak baru belajar,
Kalau salah tolong tunjukkan.

WITH THAI AND TAMIL NAMES

COLOUR ILLUSTRATIONS

YUSOFF HAJI MOHD. SAMAN

LONGMAN

LONGMAN MALAYSIA SDN. BERHAD
Wisma Damansara, Jalan Semantan, Kuala Lumpur
25 First Lok Yang Road, Singapore 2262

*Associated companies, branches and representatives
throughout the world*

1st Published 1975
Reprinted 1981

ISBN 0 582 72409 0

Set in $\frac{11}{13}$ pt Imprint (Hot Metal)
PRINTED IN SINGAPORE BY BAN WAH PRESS

CONTENTS

LIST OF PLATES

The colour plates have been drawn by Yusoff Haji Mohd. Saman. The line drawings in the text are by the author and Yusoff Haji Mohd. Saman.

ACKNOWLEDGEMENTS

ALTHOUGH I have seen the plants and fruits which I have described, in their living state, it is impossible to compile an account such as this without great help from others. Many of the following were acknowledged in my first book *Malayan Fruits* published in 1967, but as I have been able to make use of a great deal of the earlier material I would like to thank them once again.

I am indebted to the Ministry of Agriculture for the assistance given to me in providing specimens and for the use of the library and herbarium; to the Forest Research Institute at Kepong, and especially to Mr. J. Wyatt-Smith for his assistance, advice and suggestions.

Once again I have drawn heavily on *Wayside Trees of Malaya* by E. J. H. Corner, whose vast knowledge of the trees of this country is preserved in this publication, which is recognised as one of the finest of its kind. I have in the main followed his nomenclature for botanical names.

Equally I have relied on *A Dictionary of the Economic Products of the Malay Peninsula* by I. H. Burkill, whose fascinating and readable account of the history and uses of Malaysian fruits has been invaluable.

I am grateful once again to the Director of the Royal Botanic Gardens, Kew, for identification of specimens and to Mr. Forman especially for help with nomenclature; to the Botanic Gardens, Singapore, and to Mr. K. C. Cheang, Horticultural Officer at Penang Botanic Gardens, for much help with specimens; and also to my husband, for reading the manuscript and for patiently trying out the more obscure local fruits.

To all the many people who have helped in some way or other, especially the Malays in rural kampungs who have on so many occasions charmingly taken a stranger into their midst to explain uses of fruits and point out the rarer species – to them I am grateful.

BETTY MOLESWORTH ALLEN

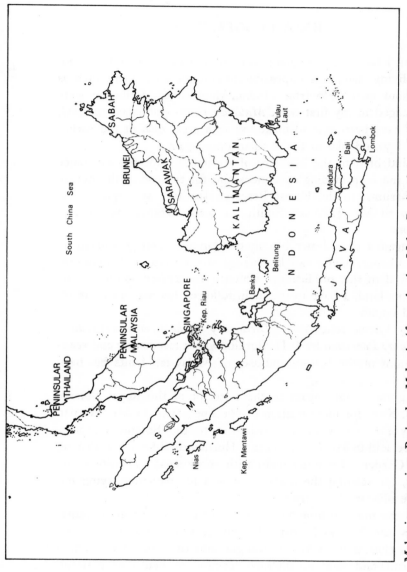

Malaysia comprises *Peninsular Malaysia* (formerly the Malay Peninsula) and *East Malaysia*, which includes Sarawak and Sabah.

Singapore and *Brunei* are separate countries. Sumatra, Java and most of Borneo (Kalimantan) are part of *Indonesia*.

INTRODUCTION

In Malaysia and Singapore we are indeed fortunate to have a climate in which plants grow rapidly and lushly, and although it may not be sufficiently dry nor cool for many of the well known foreign fruits to grow, we do cultivate many other excellent fruits. There is, however, in some of the northern states of West Malaysia, a more definite dry season and a cooler, wetter one, and here the Grapefruit, Custard Apple and Oranges grow. In many other states as well, one sees the cherry-like fruits of Rukam, and the related Lovi-lovi or Rukam manis which is more common in Singapore.

In the hill-stations the Purple Passionfruit, Loquat and Tree Tomato are successfully cultivated.

Generally speaking there are two main fruiting seasons, the heaviest being between June and August, and the second between November and February depending on the climatic conditions of that year. Many of the plants are seasonal and fruit during these periods whilst others bear more or less continuously.

This short account includes the more commonly cultivated fruits which are sold in the markets throughout Malaysia and Singapore. Fruits imported from temperate climates, and which do not normally grow here, have been omitted although they are also seen in shops and the market places.

Some of the fruits described are native to this part of the world and wild trees are to be found in our forests. Many, however, have been brought here from other tropical countries, some of them centuries ago by traders and settlers, and are now part of the countryside; it is often difficult to believe that they are not truly native. Some of the more familiar came from South America and include the Papaya, Pineapple, Guava, Chiku and Durian Belanda. Although there are plenty of native mangoes, the Indians introduced some of the long-fruited forms, and the Water Apple and probably the Jackfruit are Indian natives. The Pomegranate came from Persia, and possibly tropical Africa provided the Watermelon; but so many have been in cultivation for such a long time that their origins are lost in the mists of time.

1

Although there is no doubt that we are greatly indebted to other countries for good fruits we must not underrate those that are native. These include the Mangosteen, Durian, Rambutan and Pomelo, and possibly most of the Bananas. These compare most favourably with the foreign fruits and added to this, some remain typically South East Asian for, being intolerant of long dry seasons, they are seldom cultivated successfully elsewhere.

All these native and quasi-native fruits which grow so commonly all through Malaysia and Singapore, play a very important part in the diet of these countries. It is a pity therefore that the imported Apples, Grapes and Pears are so popular and too often considered to be more beneficial than those grown in this country. Perhaps because they are expensive, a snob value has been built up around them.

Of great significance is a recent Malaysian Government survey on vitamins in fruit, for this has shown that many of the local fruits contain a much higher percentage of vitamin C than the imported fruits. Papaya, Guava, and Limes for instance, have 70 mg of vitamin C, whilst Rambutan, Durian and Carambola have only a little less. In the same chart, Grapes, Plums and Pears have no more than 10 mg, and Apples just under 20 (the same as Bananas).

The average countryman cultivates and uses the local fruits, but it is the town dweller, who needs encouragement to use more of these and less of the imported fruits. It cannot be stressed too often that one of the cheapest market fruits, the Papaya, is one of the most nutritious, especially for children.

Throughout the country there are usually many different Malay names for one fruit and it has not been possible to include more than a few. Now that there is so much travelling into the once-isolated areas, these interesting regional names may well disappear and so there is an urgent need for them to be recorded whilst they are still remembered. In the past there has been great variation in the spelling of Malay words but this book follows the agreed Malaysian-Indonesian usage now common throughout the region.

In view of the confusion which often arises between the political and scientific use of the term Malaysia the map below should be of assistance in distinguishing the different political areas referred to in the text.

PART ONE

DICOTYLEDONS

Mango and Poison Ivy Family (*ANACARDIACEAE*)

To this family belong some well-known fruits, as well as some of Malaysia's most poisonous trees. The cultivated fruit trees include the Mangoes, Kundangan, the Kedondong and the Amra or Hog Plums. The poisonous trees are called Rengas and have very irritant sap which may severely blister the skin. Some of these trees resemble the mangoes, but luckily are nearly all found in heavy forest and not in cultivation.

Mangoes all come from *Mangifera* trees whose true home is in South East Asia. Centuries ago the Portuguese took them to tropical Africa where in Mombasa and Zanzibar, for instance, they are now part of the landscape and often thought to be native. All parts have resinous sap which in some species causes irritation to the skin. Fruits are produced twice a year, sometimes more often. They may be eaten tidily if cut around the middle to the stone and the upper section gently revolved and lifted off.

Indian Mango: Mangga (*Mangifera indica*)   Plate 1
Thai: Ma-muang.   Tamil: Manga or Mangas
The tree grows to about 80 feet and becomes woody and untidy with age. The sap is almost completely harmless. Leaves vary greatly in size from about 6 to 15 inches and have long drawn-out tips pointing downwards; flowers are fragrant. Fruits vary enormously in size and shape from almost round ("Pauh" shaped) to narrow oblong or oval ("Mempelam") and are slightly beaked at one side. When ripe the skin may be yellow or orange-coloured with a red flush, or greenish-yellow; the flesh is bright yellow, very juicy and sweet, and sometimes with an aromatic smell. The stone is covered with fibres, but in good cultivated forms, the fibres are short.

This is our best known Mango and the fruit is polymorphic. Often the best flavoured, long fruits sold in the markets about April and May and later in the year, come from Thailand, Burma or India. These are usually yellow-flushed with red. They are however, rare compared with the native ones which are so common in the Malaysian markets.

This mango is one of the oldest of our cultivated tropical fruits and has been known for over 4,000 years. We are not sure which country it originally came from, but this species does need a more definite dry period than Malaysia has in order to produce really good fruits. The Malay name probably came from the Tamil which is Sanskrit in origin.

KUINI: (*Mangifera odorata*)   Plate 2
Thai:Ma-mut (It is also used for another mango, the Binjai).
This is a tree similar in height to Mango, and the sap has a strong resinous smell but is practically harmless. The unripe fruits, however, contain a poisonous sap and so should not be eaten until fully ripe. Leaves vary in size from about 6 to 14 inches and have a short tip; flowers are strongly fragrant and the fruits are oval, up to 5 by 4 inches, and usually without an obvious point. The skin is green or yellowish-green and the flesh is a light orange colour, juicy and sugary sweet. Nearly always the ripe fruit has a strong smell, but not unpleasantly so, and the stone is covered with soft fibres.

Kuini is probably native to West Malaysia. It is a very common tree in lowland orchards and great piles of the greenish fruits are a common sight in the local markets. It could be confused with another mango which is also very common. This is Bachang (*Mangifera foetida*) whose fruits are not usually eaten raw. The fruits are rather short and fat and have a slight point at one side; the skin colour is greenish and there is a very fibrous stone. The flesh is yellow and the sap is extremely irritant. The fruits have a strong turpentine smell, yet the tree is commonly cultivated and the fruits are sold in the markets for use in curries and chutney.

CHERIMOYA FAMILY (*ANNONACEAE*)

The fruit of this tropical family is botanically interesting, for in

4

the genus *Annona* the flower contains several ovaries most of which develop and coalesce into one large fruithead. This may be called an "aggregate" fruit which differs from the "collective" fruit of the Cempedak and Jackfruit (p. 23) although they may look similar. Leaves are always simple and are alternate on the twigs, and the flowers have thick, fleshy petals arranged in two layers, 3 inner and 3 outer.

Three species of *Annona* from tropical America are frequently cultivated in Malaysia and Singapore for their fruits. These are small trees or shrubs and the best known is the Durian Belanda. The other two, the Sugar Apple (*A. squamosa*) and the Custard Apple (*A. reticulata*), more common on the East Coast and in the north of the Peninsula, are not really suited to the moist equatorial climate of Malaysia. The Sugar Apple, however, is common in Thailand, where is called Noi-na.

SOURSOP: DURIAN BELANDA (*Annona muricata*)
Thai: Thu-rian-khaek
Tamil: Seetha
A small, quick-growing, evergreen tree not more than 25 feet tall; when old it becomes straggly and untidy. It is not related to the Durian. Leaves are about $2\frac{1}{2}$ – 7 inches long and not more than 3 inches wide, and are medium green and glossy. The flowers are up to $1\frac{1}{2}$ inches wide, are greenish and hang from short stalks from the trunk, thick branches and twigs; they have a strong, unpleasant smell. Fruits are 5–10 inches or more in length and vary in shape, but are nearly always longer than wide and often somewhat kidney-shaped. The colour is darkish green (yellow when over-ripe), and the skin is covered with soft green prickles which are curved and about $\frac{1}{4}$ inch long. There is often a constriction like a fault, where the skin has not swollen evenly and the prickles are much closer together. When ripe the fruit is soft and bruises very easily; the skin is thin and the flesh white and pulpy and has a pleasant, not strong smell. There are many black, shining seeds about $\frac{3}{4}$ inch long loosely embedded in the pulp.

The Soursop was taken to other tropical countries ages ago, and has certainly been in Malaysia for several centuries. It is now common throughout the country and fruits extremely well in Singapore.

Fig. 1 Soursop: Durian Belanda

PAPAYA FAMILY (*CARICACEAE*)

Papaya is such an odd plant of the vegetable world that it is given a
family of its own. Botanically it is a large herb with no hard, woody
tissues such as are found in the trunks of other trees. It is native to
tropical America, but has been in cultivation for a very long time.

Papaya is commonly spelt this way, but perhaps correctly should be Pepaya. The name "Pawpaw" is used instead in some countries such as Australia and Africa, but in parts of the United States this name is given to another plant, related to the Durian Belanda rather than to the Papaya.

PAPAYA (*Carica papaya*)   Plate 3
Pawpaw; Tree Melon; Ketela; Kepaya
Thai: Ma-la-ko
Tamil: Pappali
A soft-tissued and extremely rapid-growing plant which is evergreen and hairless. There is normally one trunk which may grow to 30 feet in height and crowned by a tuft of leaves. The trunk is hollow, straight and the skin is smooth, apart from being scarred by fallen leaf stalks. A milky juice is present in most parts of the plant. The leaves are large and thin and alternately arranged around the trunk near the top. They are deeply lobed and often about 2 feet long and wide; the stalk is *jointed* to the trunk, falling off cleanly when old. Flowers are whitish or cream with waxy petals, and are sweet-smelling. A plant may have only male flowers or only female, or, more commonly, there may be some with both stamens and styles.

The *male* flowers are smaller than the female (about 1–1½ inches long) and there are several clustered together on a stalk. There will be several of these on one long flower-stalk, about 1–3 feet long, drooping from the trunk. The flower itself is stalkless and there are 5 petals joined together for most of their length with 10 stamens attached near the top of the flower. On a male tree there may be an occasional female flower at the end of a bunch of male flowers and small round fruits, about 4 inches wide, may result. *Female* flowers are larger, up to 2½ inches long, and the 5 petals are large and quite separate. They enclose a large pale ovary which is capped by 5 flat, lobed stigmas. These flowers are usually solitary but there may be 2–3 together on very short stalks, and they are always in the axils of the leaf-stalks against the trunk, never in long stalked clusters. A young female plant may have a few sterile or partly male flowers, and these do not set fruit. There are however, many inter-mediate stages between the male and female and nearly all of these produce fruit, some resulting in very good strains.

7

The fruits sold in the markets vary greatly in size, shape and flavour. The size is commonly about 8 to 14 inches long; they are usually roughly oblong, blunt at the ends or slightly pointed at the apex. The skin is smooth, thin, and at first is green covered with a greyish bloom; it ripens to yellow or an orange colour, or flushed with red. A rarer form has cream coloured skin even when unripe. Inside, the flesh varies from creamy-yellow to a tomato red; the central part is hollow and on its walls attached by tiny, short pale threads, are many small seeds which are wrinkled and black.

In West Malaysia the flavour of the fruit is usually very delicate, but in Thailand, northern India and Africa where there is a cool season, Papaya has a much stronger flavour.

The Spanish brought this plant to the Philippines centuries ago from Tropical America, and it must have been soon after that it came to Malaysia, for we know from the writings of a traveller, of a *Papaios* in Malacca in the 16th century. Papaya is very commonly cultivated throughout Malaysia and Singapore. Raw fruits *are extremely high in vitamin A and possess as much calcium as the best oranges, and this increases with ripeness.

PUMPKIN FAMILY (*CUCURBITACEAE*)

Nearly all the plants belonging to this family have weak stems and climb by means of tendrils. It contains many plants most useful to man, including the melons, gourds, cucumbers and pumpkins, which are cultivated throughout the world.

WATER MELON: SEMANGKA (*Citrullus lanatus*)
(In Malaysia alone there are many local names; only a few are given here).
Beteka, Kemendikai, Mendikai (Johore), Tembikai (Perak), Timun Tembikai.
Thai: Taeng-mo. Indonesia: Betek.
A pale green vine with soft weak stems which are easily damaged. The whole plant is softly hairy. A tendril, leaf and flower all arise

---

*See Introduction page 2.

8

Plate 1 INDIAN MANGO (*Mangifera indica*)

0   2   4   6

cm

Plate 2 KUINI (*Mangifera odorata*)

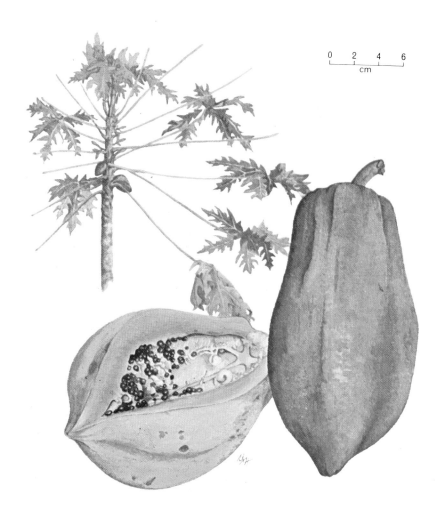

0   2   4   6
cm

Plate 3 PAPAYA (*Carica papaya*)

Plate 4 RAMBAI (*Baccaurea motleyana*)

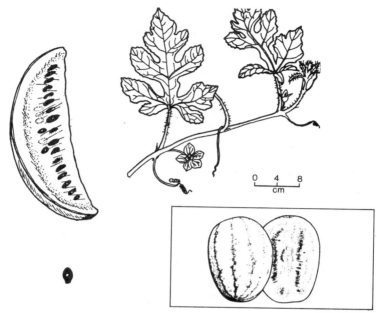

Fig. 2 Water Melon: Semangka

from one place on the stem. A tendril is about 2 inches long or more and is divided into two short arms. Leaves are very soft, pale green and dull and may be about 6 by 4 inches or larger; they are deeply lobed to within $\frac{1}{4}$ inch of the midrib and there are 2–3 lobes, which are again lobed and the margins are toothed. There is a leaf-stalk 1–2$\frac{1}{2}$ inches long. Normally the male and female flowers are produced separately. First come the male; both are yellow and about one inch wide and solitary. The male flowers have 3 stamens; the females have a pale green ovary, like an oval swelling, below the petals. Fruits vary enormously in size. When ripe they may be oblong or round, and in Malaysia are commonly between 6 and 12 inches long and are pale green splashed with dark green over the smooth skin. The flesh is bright pink and watery with soft, thin fibres running through it. There are several rows of almost black seeds evenly embedded in the flesh. The pink flesh is sweet but with little flavour compared with those growing in cooler climates.

Water Melon is native to Africa. It is not known when it arrived in India nor whether a form of it is really native there, for it is one of the very early cultivated plants grown in ancient Egypt. It has been estimated to have arrived in China by the 10th century AD, but certainly arrived in Malaysia at a much later date. The climate in this country, and in Singapore is too moist for the plant to be a great success, nevertheless it seems to be commonly cultivated and large fruits are sold in the markets.

RUBBER TREE & CASTOR OIL FAMILY (*EUPHORBIACEAE*)

This is an extremely large family of plants spread all over the world, but is most common in the tropics. Many contain a poisonous sap which is often white; in spite of this, there are many plants of economic value which bring wealth to the countries cultivating them. The Rubber Tree (Getah) from South America so extensively grown in Malaysia, and the Tapioca (Ubi Kayu or Cassava) common throughout South East Asia, are two examples. Several of our fruit trees belong here; the Larah (*Baccaurea griffithii*) is a native tree of the forests and has round, brown-skinned fruits of excellent flavour. It is seldom cultivated but the fruits are brought into the markets by the country folk. There are other fruit trees commonly cultivated, but the fruits are not eaten raw.

RAMBAI (*Baccaurea motleyana*)   Plate 4
Menteng; Thai: Ma-fai-farang.   Aborigine: Paloh
A heavy-looking, evergreen tree growing up to 60 feet in height. It is densely leafy with a round crown and is conspicuous in fruit, for these hang down in strings from the twigs, main branches, and to a lesser extent from the trunk. Leaves are simple, large, about 6–13 by 3–6 inches, and are dark green and smooth. The flowers are very small and have no petals; male and female are always on separate trees. They are pale yellowish-green and sweetly scented, and are scattered on a hanging, thin stalk 10–30 inches or more long. The fruits form on these communal stalks on the female tree; they are usually slightly longer than wide, about 1–1¾ inches by 1 inch and are pale brownish-yellow. The skin is smooth, thin but velvety and

10

when ripe has soft, translucent and whitish flesh. There are 2–5 pale brown seeds, each about ½ inch long.

Rambai is native to Malaysia and is commonly cultivated in the lowlands. It is also native to Borneo, Sumatra, Java etc., where cultivated trees are common. The fruits are most pleasant and refreshing; they are eaten raw and mounds of them are seen in the markets during the season. Trees are intolerant of cool weather so they are seldom, if ever, grown successfully outside South East Asia. In the north of the Peninsula, the name Rambai is given to some other species of native *Baccaurea*.

Rambai fruits are easily confused with Duku and Langsat, and the following guide may help to distinguish them:

RAMBAI FRUITS	DUKU & LANGSAT (see p. 20)
Fruits spaced on long stalks.	On short stalks, bunched together.
When ripe, soft to the touch, wrinkled with age.	Firm, not becoming wrinkled.
Seeds brown, flat.	Seeds green, thick (or absent).
Sepals narrow, sharp-pointed, separate from each other, longer than wide.	Sepals rounded, joined together, not longer than wide.

GAMBOGE FAMILY (*GUTTIFERAE*)

To this tropical family belong the Penaga or Ironwood Tree (*Mesua ferrea*) and the Penaga Laut (*Calophyllum inophyllum*), both common roadside trees in Malaysia. The tropical American Mammee Apple is also in this family, and the tree which produces the gamboge of commerce is closely related to the Mangosteen. In Malaysia the most important are the many species of *Garcinia* which produce good fruits. Apart from the Mangosteen there are the Mundu, the Kandis and Cerapu which are still frequently cultivated in Malay kampungs and which produce sweet edible fruits. The flowers in this family are either male or female and are found on different trees. There are 4–5 large sepals (which remain on the fruits) and 4–5 petals,

11

usually brightly coloured, many stamens on the male flowers and on the female the stigma is flat, pimply or lobed, and this is an important character when distinguishing the species.

MANGOSTEEN: MANGGIS (*Garcinia mangostana*)   Plate 5
Sementah, Mesta (east coast)
Thai: Mang-khut.   Tamil: Mangustai
   *Hendakkan buah si manggis hutan, Masak ranum tergantung tinggi.**

An evergreen tree of medium height, evenly and densely leafy. The sap is yellow and the trunk is straight, the branches low and arched. Leaves are simple and opposite, a pair being at a different angle from the next. They are commonly about $7 \times 3\frac{1}{2}$ inches, dark green or olive green, but pink when very new. Flowers are large and solitary or in pairs at, or near the twig ends, amongst the leaves. They are about $1\frac{1}{2}$ to 2 inches wide, rather fleshy-looking with 4 large curved sepals and 4 petals; the latter, together with at least two of the sepals, are flushed with pink or red. A flower opens in the late afternoon, the petals fall rapidly, but the sepals remain, resembling petals. Only trees with female flowers are known in cultivation and the fruit is formed in a peculiar way without fertilisation. Actually in a flower there are several tiny stamens, but they are sterile. Fruits are round, $2\frac{1}{2}$–3 inches across with a smooth, firm rind, pale green at first, ripening to purple or crimson-purple. The apex is crowned with 5–8 flat lobes of the stigma which are now woody, and the rind, about $\frac{1}{4}$ inch thick, is deep red and fibrous, and stains hands and clothes. In the centre of the fruit there are 5–8 fleshy segments which are startlingly white, and some contain a large light brown seed. Mangosteen is eaten raw, and the flavour of these segments is delicate and slightly acid. It is one of the most delicious of all the tropical fruits.

Mangosteen is indigenous to this part of the world and wild trees have been found in the jungle on the east coast. Trees are very commonly grown throughout Malaysia and Singapore.

---

*The proverb suggests that, although the object is difficult to obtain, it may be achieved if sufficient effort is made.

Asam Gelugur (*Garcinia atroviridis*)

Thai: Som-maw-won

A distinctive narrow tree growing to about 60 feet in height with drooping branches, twigs and leaves. The sap is colourless and twigs are smooth, green and not angled. Leaves are commonly about 8 by 2½ inches, long and narrow with a pointed tip and upturned edges. They are dark green and glossy, and new leaves are bright pink; all of them drooping in a limp way. The female flowers, about 1¼ inches wide, have 4 cherry-red, slightly convex petals surrounding a thick green ovary which is capped by a dull brick-red stigma. Fruits are solitary on the twig ends and hang down with their weight. They are about 3–4 inches wide and fluted from top to bottom with 12–16

Fig. 3 Asam Gelugur

13

deep grooves. The apex is flattened, the centre being hollow and dark; the skin between the flutings is smooth and thin, it is green at first ripening to a bright orange-yellow. The texture is firm even when ripe and the flesh is the same orange colour.

Ripe fruits are acid and astringent in taste, but are eaten with savoury foods. They are also sliced and sun-dried, being commonly seen on flat trays on roadsides in the north; these are used in Malay curries. Asam Gelugur is native to West Malaysia and Burma and is commonly cultivated in kampungs, being very common from Perak northwards and it is also common in Thailand. Although the fruit is not eaten raw as other fruits, it has been included for the narrow tree with drooping branches is conspicuous even without the orange fruit and it is commonly seen on roadsides.

Cinnamon Family (*LAURACEAE*)

A large tropical family of trees and shrubs with Bay Laurel (Sweet Bay) reaching the sub-tropics. It includes many beautiful trees, good timber as well as Camphor and Cinnamon, and the family is well represented in Malaysian forests. The flowers are greenish or greenish-yellow, very small, but their structure is most interesting.

Avocado (*Persea americana*)
Buah Mentega (this is also used for another Malaysian fruit). Alligator Pear.
Thai: A-wo-kha-do. Tamil: Anakoya-pallam
A medium-sized evergreen tree sometimes growing to about 40 feet in height. The leaves are simple, spirally arranged, but bunched together towards the twig ends. They are commonly about 4 by 2 inches and are firm in texture, hairless when mature, and yellow to medium green and slightly shiny above, but whitish green and dull below. Flowers are about ½ inch wide, greenish with a pleasant scent. They have no petals but there are 6 downy sepals which resemble them. Of the 12 stamens, only 6 to 9 are fertile and there is one thin, hairlike style. Fruits vary in shape and colour. When ripe they may be yellowish or deep green minutely speckled with white, or purple with green streaks or just deep purple. The skin is shiny, hairless

and thin and the fruit feels soft when ripe. Shapes may be from quite round to oblong and narrowed at the stalk end; in size they are usually between 4–7 inches by 3–4 wide in Malaysia, but new strains with different kinds of fruit are being planted continually. Flesh is soft, yellowish to a light green, and has the consistency of butter. There is one large, round seed loosely enclosed in a central cavity; it is warty and covered with a brown papery skin. Fruits hang on pendulous stalks from the woody twigs, often several in a bunch.

A native of tropical America, the Avocado is much cultivated in warm and tropical countries, but is a comparative newcomer in Malaysia. The fruit has an extremely high food value, for it is rich in vitamins and possesses probably more proteins than any other known fruit, and of course has a very high fat content. The history of its cultivation goes back to the Aztecs, where in the ancient Mayan civilisation it was called *Ahuacatl* which became *Avocado* of the Spanish settlers.

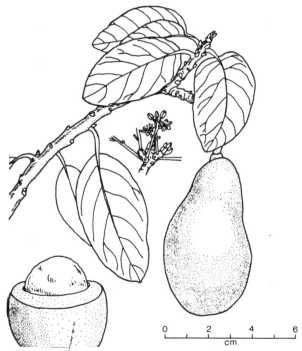

Fig. 4 Avocado

15

Loosestrife Family (*LYTHRACEAE*)

Although Pomegranate is sometimes placed in a family of its own (Punicaceae) it is more usual to include it in this one. In Malaysia the Bungor (*Lagerstroemia*) is a well-known garden and avenue tree, with attractive mauve or pink flowers and some of the smaller species, called Crepe Myrtle in other countries, are relatives. The Henna-tree or Inai (*Lawsonia*) also belongs here; it is a shrub which is cultivated in Malaysia and Singapore for its fragrant flowers. The family is widely spread throughout the world and some of the smaller plants with pink or lilac flowers are grown in gardens in Europe.

POMEGRANATE: (*Punica granatum*)
Delima; Thai: Thap-thim.   Tamil: Madalan-kai
A straggly, thin and sparsely-leaved shrub growing (in Malaysia) to about 12 feet high. The twigs and branches interlace and there are short thorns on the old wood formed by the remains of side twigs. Leaves are simple, in pairs or bunched together on small twigs; they are small, ½ to 3 inches long and up to ¾ inch wide. They are light to medium-green and shiny above and the stalks are short and usually red. Flowers are most conspicuous, being about 2 inches wide and scarlet, very occasionally white. They may be solitary or there may be several together on short stalks near the twig ends. The calyx is scarlet and has 5–9 short, pointed lobes. There are 5–8 scarlet petals which are crumpled and veined, each about ¾ inch long, these surround a brush of yellow-tipped stamens. Fruits are borne at and near the ends of long twigs of semi-mature wood, which are usually leafless by then. They are round and up to 4 inches or so across, and have a hard smooth skin which is greenish in colour, but with a red flush even when immature. The calyx lobes remain in a crown on the top of the fruit. (Those seen in Malaysian markets are often imported, and are slightly larger and golden yellow suffused with red). When cut the rind is bright yellow about ¼ inch thick and inside this are several compartments which contain many smallish seeds; these are surrounded by rose-pink to red transparent flesh, which is juicy. The seeds about ¼ inch long are white and these and the flesh are eaten.

Pomegranate is of such ancient cultivation that it is now well scattered throughout the tropics and warmer climates of the world. Originally from Persia, it was known centuries ago and is famous in Greek mythology; in ancient Egypt it was illustrated in paintings and sculptures; was one of the shrubs of the Hanging Gardens of Babylon. It also features in ancient coats of arms of cities in Spain and Turkey. Fruits were carried on caravan journeys through the deserts, for the flesh being slightly astringent, is an excellent thirst quencher, and because of its tough rind, the fruit travels well.

The Persian name for Pomegranate is Dulim or Dulima and the Sanskrit is Dadima or Dalim, and it is from these that the Malay name has been derived. It has been cultivated in Malaysia for many centuries and is still very common here.

Fig. 5 Pomegranate

MALLOW & HIBISCUS FAMILY (*MALVACEAE*)

A large, world wide family of trees, shrubs and herbs. Many useful products are obtained from them, the most important being cotton. The fibres in many are extremely tough and are economically valuable. Kapok, obtained from the pods of tall *Ceiba pentandra* trees with the stiff right-angled branches so commonly seen in Malaysia, belongs to this family; also there are many garden plants with beautiful flowers.

DURIAN: (*Durio zibethinus*) Plate 6
Civet Fruit; Thai: Thu-rian, Rian
  Bagai mentimun dengan Durian*

A tall tree growing to about 120 feet in height, with a straight trunk sometimes widened at the base, and with almost horizontal, thick branches, placed high on the trunk. Trees are narrow in outline, especially when old. When young they are bushy and leafy almost to the ground and twigs and new growth are covered with reddish-brown scurfy scales which are shiny. Leaves drooping from the twigs are about 2½–9 by 1–3 inches and the shape is oblong or elliptic with entire margins and a pointed tip. The colour varies from a bronze-green to an almost olive-green, and they are hairless and shiny above, but below are scurfy with a coating of silvery-grey scales. Flowers are in stalked bunches, a few or many (sometimes 20) in a bunch. Each flower is large, about 2 or 3 inches long and has a distinctive smell of sour milk. They open in the afternoon at about 3 pm, and the calyx, petals and stamens fall before dawn next day. The outer covering of the flower (the calyx) is divided into two parts; the outermost which covers the bud is about 1 inch long and splits into 2 or 3 segments as the bud develops; these are scaly and greenish-bronze on the outside. There is an inner calyx joined together and has 3–5 pointed lobes; it is also scaly, but pale gold in colour. This calyx surrounds 5 or sometimes 4 petals which are white or tinged with green, but there is a form with bright red petals. There are many stamens and they are joined together in 4–5 bunches of 10 or more to a bunch.

---

*This Malay proverb refers to a test between the weak and the strong (i.e. between a cucumber and a durian).

18

Fruits are very strong smelling, large and heavy, and commonly about 8 by 7 inches, but sometimes as long as 10 inches. Usually they are a little longer than wide, but sometimes are round. They hang on thick stalks from the main and smaller branches (but not from the trunks). The colour varies from olive to yellowish–green and the rind is thick, extremely tough and covered with thick, sharp-pointed coarse spikes, each being about ½ inch long and ¾ inch wide at the base; these are slightly angled and abruptly tapered to a very sharp and hardened point. Amongst the spikes can be traced 4–5 faint depressions which run from the base to the apex of the fruit, and it is here that it splits open if left to mature naturally. There are many large seeds, each one is embedded in a rich cream or yellow coloured pulp of a custard-like consistency (the aril), and it is this pulp which is eaten. The seeds are 2–2½ inches long, covered with a thin, light brown skin; they are hard but not stony. A chemical change takes place in the pulp after the fruit has fallen, so it should be eaten within two days of gathering. They should not be split open before buying, as the pulp rapidly becomes sour when in contact with the air.

Fruits are not collected off the tree but are left to fall and in many Malay States there are still traditional laws governing the right to collect the fruit. During the height of the season, Durians are sold in the markets and often on roadside stalls, usually in the afternoon and evening. A tree will bear fruit about 5 to 7 years after planting the seed, and trees usually have two crops a year, between November and February and again from June to August, the latter being the heavier. Then the air is scented with their pervading smell.

This is undoubtedly Malaysia's most famous fruit. It is thought to have originated either in West Malaysia or Borneo, but has been cultivated for hundreds of years in tropical Asia. Probably no other fruit has had so many contradictory descriptions written about its smell and flavour. Many foreigners agree that the smell is offensive, and never taste the fruit which is so delicious. It is the smell of the outer covering that is strong, for the pulp is much more delicate. For a first attempt the pulp should be chilled and then eaten in the open air, the result being so good that it is worth persisting.

Durian is an extremely rich fruit and has a very high food value; this possibly gives it the reputation of being an aphrodisiac. Most wild animals, including the tiger, eat the fruit of the jungle trees. There are many different races of the cultivated trees for they are nearly always propagated from seed. Some of the best fruits come from Perak and Thailand. Durian cakes are commonly made and sold throughout Malaysia; these travel well and keep fresh for some months. They look like thick black sausages, and the flavour is less strong, but it is important to buy good quality cakes as the flavour tends to vary enormously; some made in Penang are considered to be amongst the best.

MAHOGANY FAMILY (*MELIACEAE*)

This is a family of trees and shrubs native to the warmer countries of the world. The wood is usually scented, leaves are alternate and divided into large or small leaflets. Many trees have very hard wood of great economic value such as the Mahogany from tropical America, and the Satinwood from India. The China-berry (*Melia azedarach*) is well known as a shade tree in temperate and tropical gardens, and is frequently used as an avenue tree. It has lilac flowers and yellow fruits. The Nim (Neem) tree of India (*Azadirachta*) also belongs here. There are three native fruits belonging to this family which are often seen in the local markets. One is Sentul or Kecapi (*Sandoricum koetjape*); these are lofty forest trees and were cultivated in the older, and larger, gardens of the past, where sometimes one may still see good specimens. The fruits are round, about 3 inches in diameter, with a thick, downy, yellowish rind and white, translucent, juicy flesh smelling of peaches. The Langsat and Duku are the other two, and these have also been grouped together under one botanical name; although the fruits are quite different, there is not really enough to separate them botanically.

LANGSAT and DUKU (*Lansium domesticum*)   Plate 7
Langseh; Thai: Lang-sat, La-sa, Du-ku (from the Malay).

LANGSAT	DUKU
Ripe fruit :	
Thin skin with milky juice.	Thick skin, no milky juice.
Shape oblong, up to 1½ inches wide.	Shape round up to 2 inches wide.

20

Fig. 6 Langsat

They are medium-sized trees, from about 25 to 50 feet in height. Langsat is usually scraggy with a narrow shape and is sparsely leafy, whilst Duku is attractively shaped with a wide crown and is densely leafy. Leaves are similar, they are large but divided into 5–7 leaflets (they may look like individual leaves) plus a terminal one and each is about 5–7 inches long. They vary from rather dark green (Langsat) to pale green (Duku). Flowers are small, about ½ inch wide and are sweetly scented. They are stalkless and there are many on a drooping communal stalk. Fruits differ conspicuously between the two forms; in Langsat there are commonly about 20 fruits on the main stalk, and about 8–12 in Duku. In both, the fruits are closely bunched together and have very short or no individual stalklets as is seen in Rambai. In some forms of Duku the flesh is pink, otherwise both are white and juicy, the flavour varying from sweet to sour and always very refreshing. There are 5 segments which easily fall apart and when seeds are present they are large and thick, and imbedded one to a segment; they have a green skin and are bitter. Duku seldom has seeds. The skin ripens to a greyish buff with brown blemishes which eventually covers the skin when over-mature. In Langsat this skin is very thin and has a milky juice, which is not present in the thick (¼ inch) skin of Duku.

Both Langsat and Duku are native to this part of the world, but have been in cultivation for a very long time. In the fifteenth century, Chinese voyagers saw these trees in Javanese villages and were hopeful of growing them in China, but were not successful. The trees will not tolerate slight cold, nor even long dry spells, and so today remain typically Malaysian. Yet they are well known overseas by reputation but foreigners coming here are apt to confuse them with Rambai so a small guide has been given on page 11.

Recent botanical work on these trees indicates that the genus should be changed from *Lansium* to *Aglaia* and new specific names have been suggested.

Fig & Mulberry Family (*MORACEAE*)

Mainly tropical, this family includes some well-known fruits such as the Mulberry, Osage Orange and the European Fig, which is now widely cultivated in many countries of the world. Species of *Artocarpus* and *Ficus* (Fig) are very well represented in Malaysia, and of the former, the well-known Breadfruit is cultivated in the north where there is more or less a dry season, but is now much less common than it used to be.

The family comprises mainly trees and shrubs; they have milky juice, with leaves usually alternate and simple or entire, and flowers so small that it is often thought they have none. The Malayan Banyan and the Bohd or Pipal-tree which may be seen growing on roadsides and in parks are the tall spectacular figs which do not have edible fruits.

This family is often included in the Stinging Nettle family (*Urticaceae*), but the modern trend is to keep them separate.

JACKFRUIT: NANGKA (*Artocarpus heterophyllus*)*   Plate 8
Jak; Nangka bubur (with soft flesh).
Thai: Kha-nun.   Tamil: Pilla-kai
> *Hendak gugur, gugurlah Nangka,*
> *Jangan menimpa si dahan Pauh;*
> *Hendak tidur, tidurlah mata,*
> *Jangan dikenang orang yang jauh.*†

                                              Malay pantun

An evergreen tree to about 50 or 60 feet in height, shapely when young and fruiting when quite small, but becoming woody and untidy when old. The trunk is straight but short, soon breaking into thick branches; new shoots, twigs and leaves are usually hairless, but if present are very short and are white (see Cempedak). There is a thick milky sap. Leaves may be up to 9 inches long by $1-4\frac{1}{2}$ inches wide, with entire margins except occasionally on extremely young plants which often are very large and lobed. They are slightly leathery, very dark green, smooth and shiny above and pale below. The leafstalk is pale and varies from about $\frac{1}{4}-1$ inch long and is hairless. There are male and female flowers and these are in separate flowerheads. Male flowerheads are on new wood amongst the leaves, or above the female. They are swollen, oblong, $1\frac{1}{2}-4$ by $\frac{3}{4}-1\frac{1}{4}$ inches at the widest part and are rather pale green at first then darkening. When mature the head is covered with yellow pollen, and falls rapidly after flowering. The female heads hang from short stalks from the

---

*Another botanical name is A. *integra*.
†Fall Nangka if you must, but not on the branches of the Pauh. Close your sleepy eyes and sleep, and do not ponder on the memories of someone far away.

mature wood, i.e. the thick woody branches and the trunk. At first they look similar to the male heads (without pollen) but soon begin to enlarge. The stalks of both male and female flower-heads are encircled by a small green ring (see Cempedak). Fruitheads hang on thick stalks from the trunk and main branches. When ripe they are roughly oblong, very large, 12–36 inches long by 10–20 inches across. The rind is pale to dark yellow and is completely covered with small slightly-angled pimples, each about $\frac{1}{4}$ inch long with a dark pointed tip. The rind is thick and inside is a central pale pithy core around which the seeds are embedded in a firm, golden-yellow flesh. In between these are packed soft fibres of the same colour (which are the unfertilised flowers). Seeds are numerous and in one longitudinal cut, 5 or 6 may be seen; these are large and brown, about $1\frac{1}{2}$ inches by 1 inch and have a transparent, gelatinous covering.

Jackfruit is probably native to India, but is of such ancient cultivation that it had become widely spread many centuries ago in this part of the world, so we have no proof of its original home. It is also cultivated in parts of the African and American tropics. It was first known to the Western world by the writings of Pliny the Elder, a naturalist who lived about A.D. 100. The name Jak or Jack is apparently derived from a Malayalam word and was used by the Portuguese when they first encountered the fruit in southern India.

Throughout Malaysia and Singapore, Jackfruit is a very common tree, although Cempedak may be more common in the rural kampung gardens. Trees are quick-growing and bear fruit when about 3 years old, but are rather large for the average modern garden. Fruits form more or less throughout the year, although crops are heavier about the middle and the end of the year. They may take three months to ripen and should be covered to prevent animals or insects destroying them. Fruits are a valuable source of food and are rich in carbohydrates with a lesser amount of calcium and phosphorus. They can be so enormous that it has been said, one large fruithead is sufficient for a meal for one family. They are mainly eaten by Indians and Malays, to a lesser extent by the Chinese. In India there are many forms of Jackfruit, but in Malayasia there are few, and the Malays divided them into two groups, those with soft flesh around the seeds, and the others which are firmer. Ripe Jackfruit has a strong smell, rather Durian-like but not so pleasant,

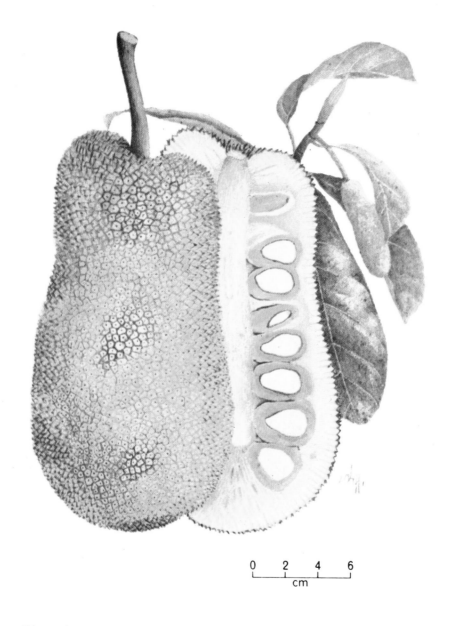

0   2   4   6
cm

Plate 9   CEMPEDAK (*Artocarpus integer*)

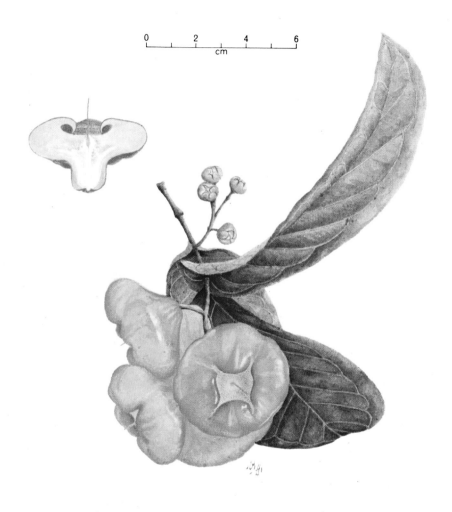

Plate 10   WATER APPLE (*Eugenia aquea*)

Plate 11   ROSE APPLE (*Eugenia jambos*)

0   2   4   6
cm

Plate 12   GUAVA (*Psidium guajava*)

perhaps. The core cannot be removed easily as in Cempedak.

The flesh around the seeds is eaten raw and a popular modern way of serving them, after removing the seed, is to chill and fill the cavity with ice-cream.

CEMPEDAK (*Artocarpus integer*)   Plate 9
Baroh (Johore); Bangong (wild forms)
Thai: Cham-pa-da

> *Daripada Cempedak baik Nangka,*
> *Daripada tidak baik ada.**   Malay proverb

An evergreen tree about 60 feet in height bearing fruit when quite small. When young it is quite often conical and shapely but it becomes woody and untidy with age. The trunk is straight but short, the bark medium-grey and most parts contain a milky sap. New shoots, leaf and flower stalks are covered with thin, wiry brown hairs which are up to ¼ inch long and have a row of similar hairs by each stipule scar, at the base of the leafstalk. Leaves are commonly about 6 by 3 inches, but some may be as much as 11 by 4½. The margins are entire or occasionally lobed in very young plants and the texture is stiff. They are medium-green and dull above usually with hairs on the midrib and main veins, and below, the veins are prominent and have stiff, sometimes, hooked brown hairs on them. The leafstalk is about 1 inch long, fringed with short stiff hairs. Flowerheads are the same construction as Jackfruit, but differ in that the male heads are smaller, thinner, up to 2 inches long by ½ inch wide, and are yellowish in colour even when immature; there is no ring on the top of the flowerhead by the stalk. Fruiting heads grow from the trunk and main branches and when ripe are roughly oblong, and may be as large as 14 by 6 inches. In colour they are golden-yellow to light brown with a thin rind which is covered with pimples; these are rather flat but vary greatly, and usually the dark tip is slightly pointed. Flesh is golden-yellow to light brown and the seeds are similar to Jackfruit's but have a loose and shiny, papery covering.

Cempedak is native to this part of the world and has been cultivated for so long that through selective breeding, fruits with thick and

---

*Similar to the English proverb "Half a loaf is better than none."

25

sweet pulp around the seeds are common in Malaysia and Singapore There are however, trees with inferior fruits, especially those growing wild in the forests. These are called Bangkong.

It is the somewhat slimy, yellow custard-like pulp around the seeds that is eaten raw. A slice is cut from the fruit, and the core is pulled out by the stalk. Seeds are also eaten but should be first cooked. The smell and taste of this fruit is very strong, also rather reminescent of Durian, but often thought to be better than Jackfruit (hence the proverb). The taste is sweeter and the food value similar. It will bear fruit about five years after germination, and requires little or no attention.

MYRTLE & EUCALYPTUS FAMILY (*MYRTACEAE*)

This enormous family is spread all over the world. It is well represented in Malaysia and Singapore, both in cultivation and in the forests. The Eucalyptus of Australia and the Myrtle of Europe are amongst the best known, and the plants which produce Cloves and Allspice belong here also.

Plants of this family have simple, opposite leaves which are nearly always aromatic. Flowers may be large or small, but are distinctive in having large numbers of stamens giving the flowers a fluffy appearance. Many cultivated in Malaysia are trees or shrubs producing edible fruits of varying quality; but only a few find their way into the markets. They are, however, commonly grown in gardens and in the kampungs. The best known are the Jambu, usually small trees, but the Kerian and Salam are large trees with small fruits and are grown in the north and on the east coast. The Surinam Cherry (Cermai belanda, *Eugenia michelii*) the small shrub with red, fluted fruits used to be common, but seems to have become unpopular in recent years. The native trees, not cultivated and with small fruits, are collectively called Kelat.

WATER APPLE: JAMBU AIR (*Eugenia aquea*)   Plate 10
Thai: Chom-phu-pa
A small and low-spreading tree, 15–25 feet high with many low branches. Leaves are large, 2–9 inches long or even more, with a

heart-shaped base clasping the twigs (stalkless). Flowers are slightly scented, about 1 inch wide, white or occasionally pinkish. They are on new wood in loose bunches. Fruits have an uneven shape, a wide apex up to $1\frac{3}{4}$ inches, and a narrow base. There is a central hollow in the apex from where the style often projects as a long, dark whisker. The colour of the fruit varies from white to bright pink, the skin is glistening, almost translucent and bruises easily. The flesh is crisp and watery, with a scented flavour, sometimes insipid.

Water Apple has been in cultivation for many centuries, originally coming from south India. It is intolerant of cold weather, so is confined to equatorial countries. The tree is quite common in Malaysian and Singapore gardens and the fruits are eaten mainly by children. Although the fruits are mainly water, the skin contains fruit sugars and a high content of vitamin A, and are good thirst quenchers; they are also very good in salads.

JAVA APPLE: JAMBU AIR RHIO (*Eugenia javanica*)
Jambu merah for pink, and Jambu hijau for green-coloured fruits. Wax apple. Thai: Chom-phu-khao

A spreading, rather open tree about 40 feet or more in height, but fruiting when quite small. The bark is pinkish, flaking off in thin pieces. Leaves are about 5–10 by $1\frac{1}{2}$–4 inches, and the base is slightly narrowed and rounded. The leafstalk is short, under $\frac{1}{4}$ inch but is distinct. Flowers are about $\frac{3}{4}$–$1\frac{1}{2}$ inches wide, almost scentless and are white or pale cream in colour. They are in clusters of 3–5 on short main stalks from the small, drooping leafy twigs. Fruits are nearly round, or wider at the apex, about 1–$1\frac{3}{4}$ inches by about 2 inches wide. At the apex there is a cavity almost enclosed by 4 thick incurving lobes. The fruit is usually pale green or whitish, but some are entirely pink or red. They are glossy, waxy and crisp to the touch, the skin is very thin and the flesh greenish or white and rather dry. The flavour is aromatic, but not unpleasantly so.

Java Apple is native here, from West Malaysia to the Andaman Islands, and is one of the most commonly cultivated Eugenias in the country, especially so in the kampungs and by shophouses. It is abundant in Java where it has been in cultivation for several centuries. It is also cultivated in tropical America and there are many different forms of fruit. The green forms are eaten with a little salt, and they

Fig. 7 Java Apple: Jambu Air Rhio

make a pleasant sauce. The pink fruits on the whole are more juicy and less aromatic, but all of them are rather flavourless. The shape of the fruits and the stalked leaves distinguish this tree from the Water Apple.

ROSE APPLE: JAMBU MAWAR (*Eugenia jambos*)*   Plate 11
Jambu air mawar, J. kelampok (when cooked).
Thai: Chom-phu-nam.   Tamil: Seeni-jambu
A small tree growing to about 20 feet with low-spreading branches

---

*In some books it is called *Syzygium jambos*.

28

and pale brown bark. Leaves are about 4–9 inches by 2½ inches and when new are shiny and pink, fading to pale green, finally dark green. They are narrow and gradually-tapered to the base and the leafstalks are about ¼ inch long. Flowers are large and showy, white to pale cream and sweetly scented, and about 3 inches wide. They are in short-stalked clusters at the ends of the newer twigs. Fruits, about 1½–2 inches wide, are almost round or a little longer than wide or slightly narrowed at the base. When ripe they may be greenish, or dull yellow flushed with pink. The skin is dull, the flesh whitish, firm and rose scented and rather dry.

Rose Apple comes from India and parts of Malaysia and has been in cultivation for centuries. It is grown throughout Malaysia, but is most common in Singapore. Fruits vary a great deal, those of poor quality being dry and tasteless. They are eaten raw or cooked with sugar, but are better mixed with other fruits, and in jams or jellies.

MALAY APPLE: JAMBU MERAH (*Eugenia malaccensis*)*
Jambu melaka: Thai: Chom-phu-sa-raek.   Tamil: Peria-jambu

A heavy-looking tree about 40–60 feet high, with a thick trunk which soon divides into large crooked branches. The bark is grey and almost corky, and the leaves are large, about 6–18 by 3½–8 inches and are bunched at the twig ends. The base is widened abruptly from the leafstalk which is short and very thick. Flowers, 2–3 inches across are very striking, for they are deep pink or cerise, and are in almost stalkless bunches on the upper part of the trunk and on bare mature wood behind the leaves (not at the twig ends). When the brightly coloured stamens fall, they lie beneath the tree for a day or two before fading completely, and make a most conspicuous carpet. Fruits are about 2–3 by 2½ inches when ripe, and are thickly oblong, or slightly narrowed at the stalk end. The skin is thin and slightly shiny, pale green at first then usually ripening to a rosy red or crimson with faint white markings. As with all the Jambu fruits there is a central hollow; the flesh is rather dry and smells and tastes of scent, yet the fruits are quite pleasant to eat.

---

*In some books: *Syzygium malaccensis*.

Fig. 8 Malay Apple: Jambu Merah

Malay Apple is certainly native to this part of the world, but the exact place is not known, for it has travelled widely, and has been cultivated throughout the moist tropics for centuries. It is now a familiar fruit tree of the American tropics and of equatorial Africa, and looks like a native tree in many of the Pacific Islands. The tree does not tolerate long dry periods, preferring constant temperatures, and thus is well suited to Malaysia and Singapore.

GUAVA: JAMBU BATU (*Psidium guajava*)   Plate 12
Jambu biji; Thai: Farang, Ma-pun, Ya-mu.
Tamil: Koiya-pallam

A small open tree growing to about 25 feet high. The bark is very smooth, pale and mottled and peels off in thin flakes. Leaves are commonly about 4 by 1½ inches, and are slightly rough to the touch, the colour is light to medium-green, and there are short leafstalks. Flowers are ¾–1¼ inches wide, one to three on short stalks by the leaf bases, and they are faintly scented. There are 5 thin white petals which fall rapidly and fewer stamens than there are in the Eugenia flowers. Fruits have a strong, sweet smell when ripe, and in Malaysia the shape and colour vary enormously. Commonly, the fruits are about 1¼–3 by 1½–2½ inches, and may be round or oblong, smooth or very faintly grooved. They are green at first ripening to greenish or lemon-yellow, or yellow flushed with pink. The skin is thin, shiny and hairless when ripe and there are many small, stony seeds which leave little room for pulp in the Malaysian forms.

Guava is a native of tropical America, but has been cultivated in other countries (including Malaysia) for centuries and has become very common. The fruits are very commonly seen in the local markets but are usually of poor quality compared with some of the tropical American cultivars. Malays noticed the resemblance to the Jambu fruits to which it is related, hence the name.

WOOD SORREL FAMILY (*OXALIDACEAE*)

Predominantly a family of the tropics and subtropics, although the Wood Sorrel is a native to the cooler parts of Europe. The *Oxalis* species are perhaps the best known, as many of these are cultivated in gardens in temperate climates. The two fruits cultivated in Malaysia come from trees, which is very unusual in this herbaceous family. The two differ greatly in general appearance, although they have a few characters in common; both are small trees with leaves divided into leaflets. There is always a terminal leaflet, so that the total number is uneven, also the smallest are at the base, near the stalk end. Flowers are small, about one inch wide or less, and are in loose clusters. In Belimbing Asam both flowers and fruit are borne mostly

31

on the trunk and woody branches, whilst in Carambola they are on leafy twigs.

Plate 13

CARAMBOLA: BELIMBING MANIS; B SEGI (*Averrhoa carambola*)
Kambola; Star-fruit. Thai: Ma-fu'ang, Fu'ang. Tamil: Tamarta
A small but shady evergreen tree, about 30 feet in height and much branched. The trunk is short and the bark smooth. Leaves are 2–7 inches long and are divided into 3–5 almost opposite pairs leaflets, which have very uneven bases, one side being broad, the other narrow. Leaves are yellowish to medium green. Flowers are small and lilac in colour and the tiny individual flower-stalks and buds are pink or red. Fruits are roughly oblong, 2–5½ inches, with 5 deep flutings or wings, running from base to apex. They are waxy, smooth and thin skinned, green at first ripening to a deep yellow. The texture is rather soft and the flesh is yellow, juicy and often sour. There may be a few pale seeds, but more often these are absent. When cut across the fruit is star-shaped.

Carambola is native to Java and possibly from Borneo to the Philippines, and has been in cultivation in South East Asia for centuries. It is now grown throughout the tropical world. Some trees produce large and fairly sweet fruits, and although they are eaten raw, they are better cooked. Fruits are very common in the local markets, for trees bear all the year round, and their distinctive shape catches the eye.

BELIMBING ASAM (*Averrhoa bilimbi*)
B'ling or Billing-billing (commonly used, apparently corruptions of the former name). Thai: Ta-ling-pring. Tamil: Bilimbikai
A small open tree growing to about 20 feet. Leaves are divided into 5–18 pairs of leaflets, and they are bunched together at the twig ends. They are pale green and the base of each leaflet is uneven, and they all droop in a characteristic manner. Fruits are narrow and unevenly oblong, about 2–3½ inches long to nearly 1 inch wide, but are usually narrowed at the stalk end. There are 5 shallow ridges running the length of the fruit, and the skin is smooth and very thin, green at first ripening pale yellowish and squashy. There are some forms which are yellow even when immature. The pulp is juicy but extremely sour.

Fig. 9 Belimbing Asam:

Belimbing Asam is native to this part of the world and is one of our commonest small fruit trees. Although, on the whole the fruits are too sour to be eaten raw, they are much used in curries, and for pickling and stewing. The juice is used to remove stains from clothes and hands. The fruits look like smooth, pale gherkins and are not likely to be confused with any other fruits in the markets.

Passionflower Family (*PASSIFLORACEAE*)

The plants cultivated in Malaysia and Singapore are native to tropical and South America and are vines, climbing by means of tendrils which curl around supports. Flowers all have a characteristic shape, are showy and scented. The seeds, inside the fruit, are imbedded in a sweet-tasting mucilage. Parts of the plant, especially the leaves, contain hydrocyanic acid and are poisonous. There are other passionfruits cultivated in West Malaysia, possibly the commonest being the Purple Passionfruit which grows at hill stations. Some of the red-flowered species are cultivated as climbers, for they do not easily set fruit in the lowlands. Another, occasionally seen, is the Giant Grenadilla (*P. quadrangularis*) with enormous greenish-yellow fruits. As with all the passionfruits, it is better to plant more than one, as flowers require cross fertilisation.

PASSIONFRUIT: BUAH SUSU (*Passiflora laurifolia*)
Buah selasih; Water-lemon; Pomme d'Or; Bell Apple; Jamaica Honeysuckle.   Thai: Sao-wa-rot
A climber with unlobed leaves, tough wiry stems, and climbing by means of tendrils. Stems are round not angled, and the tendrils grow from the leafstalk bases. Leaves are entire (not lobed as in Purple Passionfruit), are hairless and rather tough in texture, and are about 3½–5 by 1½–2½ inches. The colour varies from a medium to a yellowish-green. Flowers are large, about 2½ inches wide and have a strong pleasant scent. They hang from the stems amongst the leaves on new growth, and each has 3 large, pale green bracts capping the flower, which is spectacular, because there is a ring of long and coarse purple whiskers. These look like many stamens and are fleshy, barred violet and white, and inside this ring are the 5 separate stamens with comparatively large nodding anthers and an ovary (the immature fruit) capped by 3 knobbly styles. Fruits are oblong, about 3 × 2 inches when ripe and tapered at both ends, with a short projection at the apex. The 3 green bracts usually remain on the fruit at maturity. The skin is bright yellow or orange-yellow, smooth, dull and soft, and is sweet-smelling and the flesh is pulpy with a whitish transparent juice filled with dark seeds. The flesh is sweet with a scented flavour.

34

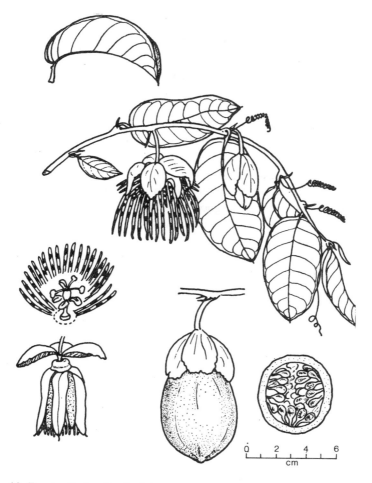

Fig. 10 Passionfruit: Buah Susu

Passionfruit was introduced into Malaysia from tropical America over two centuries ago. It now grows wild in open country especially in Singapore and Penang, and is commonly cultivated in the lowlands. Fruits are eaten raw, and when strained the juice makes a pleasant drink. Plants grow easily from cuttings and seeds and fruit continuously. The leaves are poisonous.

Citrus & Rue Family (*RUTACEAE*)

A large family from the temperate and tropical regions of the world, producing many useful fruits as well as colourful garden plants. The best known, the Citrus, are grown throughout the world in all but very cold climates. Besides the Citrus, there are other fruits cultivated in Malaysia; the Bel-fruit, Wood Apple and the Wampi used to be common, but are no longer. The Curry-leaves or Kerupulai, which are used to flavour curries, come from a bush belonging to this family. Although it is too hot for the Lemon to bear freely in West Malaysia and Singapore, the closely related Citron and the Italian Lime with large fruits make good substitutes. A green skinned orange has been cultivated with success in parts of Perak, and the Grapefruit in the far north where there is more of a monsoon climate, but the well-known cultivated oranges are imported. Limes grow extremely well in Malaysia and there are many different species and cultivated forms, but only the two most commonly used are described here.

Members of the family have been used by man for over 3,000 years, and the discovery, less than 200 years ago, that citrus fruits prevented scurvy was of tremendous importance. This dreaded disease was caused by deficiency of vitamin C and was very common amongst sailors on long sea voyages.

Flowers of the citrus are nearly always white with waxy petals and have a strong, delightful scent. The trees and shrubs are evergreen, often thorny (but may be absent in good cultivated strains). The leaves are usually simple, dark green with oil glands which may be seen as tiny transparent dots, if held to the light. Some species of citrus have strongly winged leafstalks.

Lime: Limau Asam (*Citrus aurantifolia*)

Common Lime; Limau nipis (with thin skins); L. masam; L. jerok
Thai: Som-ma-nao.   Tamil: Dhaisi-kai
A small thorny shrub growing to about 15 feet in height. Thorns are very sharp, about $\frac{1}{4}$–$\frac{1}{2}$ inch long, and are at the leaf bases. The leaf is more or less oblong, about 1–3 inches, is medium to dark green but paler or yellowish in poor soils. There is a *very narrow wing* which widens near leaf end, and these stalks are up to 1 inch long. Flowers are about 1 inch across with 4 waxy petals. Fruits,

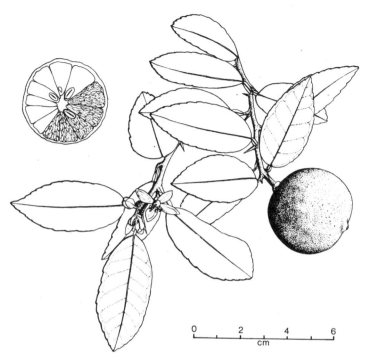

Fig. 11 Lime: Limau Asam

1–2 inches in diameter are usually round and sometimes slightly pointed. The skin varies from slightly rough and warty to smooth and shiny, and may be thick or thin. There is little pith in most forms and about 6–11 greenish segments which are not easily separable. When sold in the markets, fruits are usually green or blotched with yellow, but when left to ripen become yellow. The flesh is pale green and very acid, but may become slightly musty if the fruit is ripe.

A great many different forms and races exist of this well-known fruit, extreme forms having very thick skins and pith, with little flesh and juice. There is a form grown in Singapore which is less common in Malaysia. It is a small shrub with only a few thorns and an almost wingless leaf-stalk. Fruits are round, about 1¼ inches diameter, and the skin is coarse, thick and usually green even when ripe. The Common Lime is cultivated throughout Malaysia and Singapore in private gardens and commercially. Fruits are in great

37

demand for drinks, flavourings and pickles. The *air limau* or fresh lime drink is very thirst quenching and is to be obtained at most hotels.

Our Lime is almost identical with the West Indian Lime which originally came from this part of the world, but there the fruits have become slightly elongated. Some forms of this lime have become adapted to a short period of cool weather and can be grown in non-equatorial countries such as Egypt, Florida and parts of Mexico.

MUSK LIME: LIMAU KESTURI (*Citrus microcarpa* or possibly C. *mitis*, but there is much confusion between these species).
Limau chuit; Thai: Ma-nao-wan
A small spreading shrub to about 12 feet in height, usually thornless. Leaves have a *very narrow wing or none* and are between ¾–2½ inches long, and have a leaf-stalk of about ½ inch. Flowers are about ¼–¾ inch

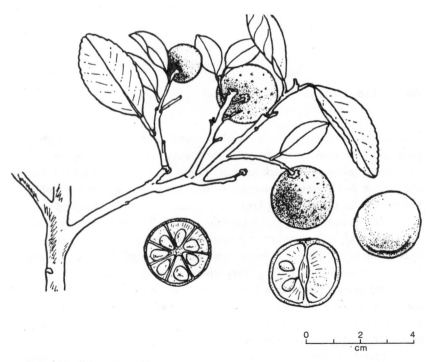

0   2   4
cm

Fig. 12 Limau Kesturi

38

wide and have 5 petals. Fruits are round, 1–1¾ inches wide with a smooth and shiny skin, green at first and washed with yellow, then finally all yellow. (When seen in the markets, they may be green). Fruits feel soft even when unripe, and the skin which is thin, peels easily. The flesh is pale to medium orange colour and is juicy and very sour. There are 6–8 segments with many large seeds.

Musk Lime must have originated in tropical Asia as it is most intolerant of the cold, and so is well adapted to Malaysian and Singapore climates. It is commonly cultivated, being perhaps most common in Perak, and fruits are produced all the year round. When ripe they have a sweet, musky smell, and make a much better drink than any of the other limes. Fruits are used enormously in food.

POMELO: LIMAU BETAWI (*Citrus grandis*)*   Plate 14
Shaddock; Limau bali; L. besar; Pampelmousse; Bali Lemon; Jerok bali (Java).
Thai: Som-o; Ma-o

A bushy tree growing to about 30 feet in height with a few or many thorns, each up to 1¼ inches long. The leaves are *winged* and are dark green and shiny and up to 6 inches long. The wings are usually about ¾–1 inch wide and the leaf-stalk up to 1 inch long. Flowers are about 1 inch wide and strongly scented. Fruits are usually very large, almost round but slightly flattened at the apex. They vary greatly in size from about 5 to 10 inches in diameter, and the skin is pale green or yellow and finely dotted with oil glands. The thickness of the skin is variable, from about ¼ to 1 inch through, and there are about 9–14 easily separated segments attached to a central pithy core. Each segment is covered with a papery white or pink skin which is easily removed. The flesh is transparent, whitish to pink or rose red, and should be sweet and juicy.

Pomelo seems to be native to Indo-China, Thailand and Malaysia, but the fruits we buy are the result of cultivation throughout the centuries. Fruits were introduced into the West Indies by a sailor called Captain Shaddock, and the name stuck. It is also used in some of the north American tropics, and in New Zealand where the tree is also cultivated.

---

*In some books the botanical name may be *Citrus maxima* or *C. decumana*.

Pomelo is one of the commonest fruits to be seen in the markets nearly all the year, and there are very many different forms. The seedless forms, and those from Thailand and Java which are considered amongst the best, quite often have pink flesh, but there are some excellent white-fleshed strains in West Malaysia too. Fruits with deep pink flesh, common in Java, have been cultivated in Florida. ' In Malaysia, there are several poor forms which have been grown from seed and others with thick white pith and bitter flesh. One of these with a downy skin grows in old cultivations in waste areas and is common in Sarawak. These fruits do not seem to be used.

Pomelo is usually eaten raw, but the Malays also preserve the rind which makes a pleasant candied peel.

LIMAU PURUT: (*Citrus hystrix*)   Thai: Ma-krut
Mention must be made of this fruit for it is very commonly seen in cultivation and in markets throughout Malaysia and Singapore, and

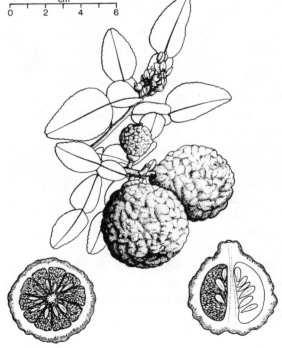

Fig. 13 Limau Purut

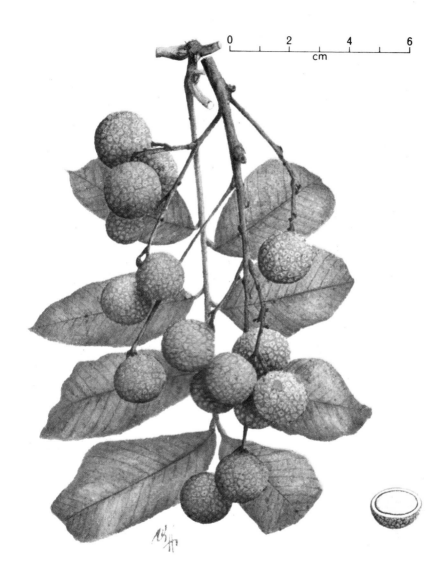

Plate 17 MATA KUCHING (*Nephelium malaiense*)

0   2   4   6
cm

Plate 18   PINEAPPLE: NANAS SARAWAK (*Ananas comosus*)

0   2   4   6

cm

Plate 19   PINEAPPLE: NANAS MORIS

0   2   4   6
cm

Plate 20   BANANA: PISANG AMBON (*Musa paradisiaca*)

the odd-looking fruits are most distinctive. They come from a small tree and the leaves appear to be divided into two, for there is a *large wing almost the size of the leaf-blade.* Flowers are white and have 4–6 pointed petals. Fruits vary in shape but are usually more or less round, and may be up to 3 inches in diameter. They are green when sold in the markets, and are usually picked from trees before they ripen. The skin is rough and warty and in most forms the pith is thick, the flesh pale green with little juice and the taste bitter. The fruit is used in many ways, mainly in cooking and in washing the hair, and in Thailand the leaf is also used in food. The rough knobs over the eyes of a crocodile are called *Limau purut Buaya.*

Litchi & Soapberry Family (*SAPINDACEAE*)

Mainly tropical and sub-tropical family of trees, shrubs and climbers, and is well represented in West Malaysian jungles. Those cultivated for their fruits, belong with one exception, to the genus *Nephelium* to which the famous Litchi belongs. This fruit is imported into Malaysia mainly dried, for the tree is not suited to our seasonless climate. There are jungle trees which produce small fruits eaten by the aborigine folk, Redan and Lotong are perhaps the best known. Mertajam is placed in another genus (*Erioglossum*); it is often cultivated in country villages and has very small fruit. In *Nephelium* the leaves are large and divided into 2–5 pairs of leaflets without a terminal one. The leaflets are usually large, but the flowers are very small and produced in large trusses. For cultivation more than one should be grown as a tree may have only male flowers and then of course would not have fruit. More frequently, however, flowers are both male and female.

RAMBUTAN: (*Nephelium lappaceum*)   Plate 15
Rambutan gading (for yellow-skinned fruits); R. lèjang (with more easily separable seeds).   Thai: Ngo; Phruan
A bushy and wide-crowned tree which grows to about 60 feet in height; the bark is dark brown and blotched with minute specks. Leaves are up to 16 inches long but divided into 2–4 pairs of leaflets which are usually alternate. Each leaflet is about 3–9 by $1\frac{1}{2}$–$3\frac{1}{2}$ inches

and is dark green and slightly shiny above. The margins are entire and often upcurled from the midrib. Flowers are very small, much less than ¼ inch wide, and are in long stalked panicles near the twig ends, amongst the leaves. They are greenish and have a pleasant smell. Fruits hang in bunches on their woody stalks on the outside of the tree. Each is large, oblong or nearly round, about 2–2½ by 2 inches; they are green at first ripening to scarlet or crimson red, or in some forms, yellow. Even when green they are conspicuous for the rind is covered with thick, curved fleshy whiskers which are red or yellow. The actual skin is quite thin and pliable and is not attached to the flesh which is firm, white and translucent. It is sweet and juicy, extremely pleasant with a mild flavour. There is one large central seed attached firmly to the flesh, but is not stony and has a light brown skin.

Rambutan is one of the commonest and best loved fruits and is native to this part of the world, to West Malaysia itself, but has been cultivated in southeast Asia for a long time. Early Arab traders took the fruit to Zanzibar, where trees are still cultivated. Outside the equatorial tropics however, Rambutan cultivation is restricted by its intolerance of cold weather. In Malaysia and Singapore it is grown in gardens and around the kampungs, and orchards of them are visible from roadsides. Trees have been found in the jungle, especially in central Malaya and many aboriginal names exist for both trees and fruit.

Rambutan fruits twice a year, occasionally more often, the main season being in the middle of the year. It is a most attractive sight to see the trees weighed down with bunches of scarlet fruits, and piles of them in the markets and on roadside stalls; there is another, shorter season in December. Fruits have quite a high content of ascorbic acid; they are normally eaten raw, either cut around the middle, or twisted between the thumb and forefinger, the skin then comes off easily. The flesh is eaten but not the seed.

PULASAN: (*Nephelium mutabile*)   Plate 16
Gerat; Thai: Ngo-khonsan
The tree is similar to Rambutan if a little smaller, and the leaflets are narrower. Leaves have 2–5 pairs of leaflets which are about 2½–7 inches long and up to 2 inches wide. Fruits are oblong, about 2–2½

by 1½ inches, often with a small undeveloped fruit attached to the stalk by the ripe fruit. The skin is very dark red when ripe and is covered with short, rather pointed knobs which are thick and fleshy but not elongated as in the Rambutan fruit, and the seed does not stick to the flesh but is easily detachable. The flesh is transparent, whitish or rather yellow and the flavour very sweet.

Pulasan is native to West Malaysia, Sumatra etc. but has been cultivated for many years. Wild trees are occasionally found in lowland forest, especially in Perak. There are several different races grown, which produce varying qualities of fruit, and there is a seedless form in Thailand.

Fruits sometimes ripen at a different time from Rambutan, a few weeks ahead or later in the year. Best crops appear after a prolonged dry spell.

MATA KUCING: (*Nephelium malaiense*)   Plate 17
Cat's Eyes (translation of the above name).
When well grown, Mata Kucing is an attractively shaped tree and could be 60 feet high, but more often is seen as a straggly small tree in kampung gardens. Leaves are divided into 3–5 pairs of drooping leaflets, but the shape and size vary enormously. A form with small blunt leaflets is common in Penang, whilst further south, for instance, in Negri Sembilan, trees often have larger, pointed leaflets about the size and shape of the Pulasan. Flowers are very small, white and scented. The fruits are round, up to ¾ inch with a tough skin which is pale, dull yellow-buff with dark, raised flecks. The flesh is whitish, translucent and sweet, but unless it is a good cultivated form, there will be only very little covering the seeds. Some forms do have flesh nearly ¼ inch thick, but it is usually less. The seed is very large in proportion and shiny brown with a pale patch at the base. Each fruit-stalk is thick but less than ¼ inch long.

Mata Kucing is native to this part of the world and has been found wild in the forests of Malaysia, Sumatra, Borneo and the Celebes. It is a handsome tree when well grown and not crowded by other trees. In West Malaysia and Singapore it is seen in orchards and around the older villages and, although rare in some areas of Perak, it is common in Penang but possibly most common of all in Negri Sembilan.

Fruits are seen in country markets but are mostly eaten by children. If bred selectively with a view to reducing the size of the seed, and thus having more flesh, Mata Kucing could become a very popular fruit, for the flavour is delightful and the seed is so easily removed. It could be used instead of the imported tinned Longan which so often accompanies a Chinese meal. They are very closely related but Longan does not fruit in Malaysia.

Gutta Percha Family (*SAPOTACEAE*)

A widely distributed tropical family which just reaches the subtropics, and is one of economic importance. It produces many edible fruits as well as the Gutta Percha of commerce, a native of Malaysia, Borneo and Sumatra. The Star Apple (*Chrysophyllum*) from tropical America has been cultivated in the north but fruits rather infrequently. The Tanjong Tree (*Mimusops*), is commonly cultivated on the east coast and in the north, on roadsides and in gardens large enough to contain them (especially in Perak), and has small fruit which is rather floury. It is native to South East Asia. The Sau or Sawah, seen on the east coast, has orange coloured fruits about $1\frac{1}{2}$ inches long which are sweet and are eaten raw. It is native but not commonly cultivated now.

The family has some common characters. There is usually milky juice in most parts of the plants; the leaves are simple and alternate, and the flowers rather small.

CIKU: SAPODILLA (*Manilkara zapota*; formerly called *Achras zapota*). Sau menila; Zapote; Naseberry.
Thai: La-mut-farang (the foreign Sau)
Tamil: Shimai-eluppai (the foreign Illipe)
An evergreen, spreading tree 30–40 feet high, with low branches and white juice. The bark is dark brown, and new shoots brown and mealy. Leaves, simple and entire are grouped together and spirally arranged at the twig ends. They are medium-green. Flowers are small and white, about $\frac{1}{2}$ inch wide but do not fully open during the day; they are strongly scented especially at night. Fruits are round or slightly longer than wide, about 2 or 3 inches long with a dull, rather

44

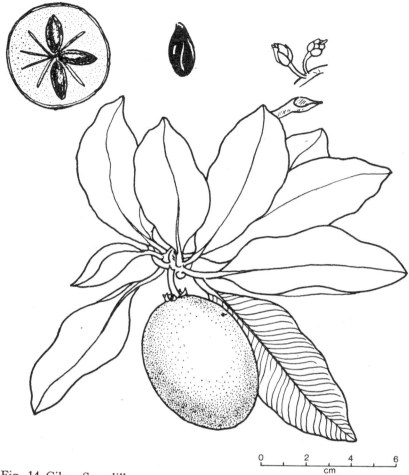

Fig. 14 Ciku: Sapodilla

mealy pale brown thin skin. When ripe, the flesh is soft, pulpy and granular. It is pinkish-brown bruising and ageing to a chestnut brown, and the flavour is delicate and very pleasant. There are usually 3–6 seeds loosely embedded in small cavities radiating in a star shape from the centre. They are hard, shiny and black.

Ciku is native to America, from southern Mexico to Venezuela, but has been cultivated in most tropical countries for many centuries.

45

Trees were well established in the West Indies by about 1500, and were also cultivated in Malaysia a long time ago. The name "Ciku" is derived from the Aztec name of Chikl. In Malaysia and Singapore this is a popular fruit tree in private gardens and orchards and is also a good shade tree. Although slow-growing it thrives in Malaysia's moist hot climate, producing fruit at frequent intervals throughout the year. Fruits are usually picked before they are ripe, but should be kept until quite mature and soft. Like many fruits, these have to be eaten just at the exact time of ripeness (just before overmaturity) to get the best flavour.

PART TWO

MONOCOTYLEDONS

Spanish Moss Family (*BROMELIACEAE*)

There are no native Bromeliads in Malaysia for the family belongs to tropical and subtropical America and the West Indies. The famous Spanish Moss which hangs from trees in the cypress swamps from Louisana to Florida belongs to this family. Many pot-plants such as *Vriesia, Billbergia* and *Pitcairnia* are also members of the family. Others produce strong fibres, and the leaves of some pineapples are used in the Philippines in making the Pina cloth. Leaves are long and strap-shaped and are clustered together; flowers are terminal.

Pineapple: Nanas (*Ananas comosus*)
Thai: Sappa-rot, Ma-kha-nat

Pineapple is one of our best known fruits and must be familiar to most people. Not so familiar, perhaps is the pineapple plant from which the fruit develops. The flowers are in heads with a terminal bunch of leaves. They are crowded together interspersed with bracts, and after fertilisation become young fruits and begin to swell. Soon there is not enough room for each to develop separately, and so they become more or less fused, the result being called a *collective fruit*. In cultivation good varieties of Pineapple seldom produce seeds, so that all reproduction must be done vegetatively, that is, planting by suckers, slips etc. At the base of the fruit, there may be leafy shoots and these are called *basal slips*. Any shoots growing from the stalk which carries the fruit are called *aerial suckers*, whilst those from the base are *basal suckers*. The tuft of leaves at the top of the fruit is called a *crown*. All of these may be used for planting, some being more successful than others in the various varieties. Although there are many forms or varieties grown in this country, the most

47

important commercial ones may be divided into four groups. Each of these has several names, as well as the individual local names.

NANAS SARAWAK and NANAS MORIS: These are the two most popular varieties sold in markets for eating raw.

NANAS MERAH and NANAS HIJAU: Used mainly for canning, less commonly eaten raw.

Plate 18

Nanas Sarawak, Sarawak Pine, Smooth Cayenne, Kew.

Leaves dark green with very distinct reddish lines running along the centre of the leaves. Leaf margins smooth or with a few prickles at the tip. Fruits medium-sized with pale yellow flesh; central woody core, thick. This is the one perhaps most commonly seen in the markets here.

Plate 19

Nanas moris, Mauritius Pine, Nanas Europa, Malacca Queen, Red Ceylon, Red Malacca.

Leaves deep green (darker than in the former) with a broad red stripe in the leaf centre and red prickles on the leaf margins. Fruits small but variable, flesh fairly bright yellow and central woody core, thin. This is the smallest but the fruit is usually very sweet and is perhaps the best one for dessert.

PLANTAIN AND BANANA FAMILY (*MUSACEAE*)

*Aku bukan budak makan pisang.** Malay proverb

This family, of great importance to man, is cultivated in nearly all tropical countries except the most arid ones, and bananas are exported to most other countries throughout the world. So it is one of the best known of all the fruits, and hundreds of names exist. Bananas must have been one of the earliest known tropical fruit crops as there are records of it having been in cultivation 4,000 years ago. By careful breeding throughout the centuries, we are able to enjoy the fine-flavoured fruits which are nearly always seedless. For

*I am no banana-eating boy. (I was not born yesterday.)

0   2   4   6

cm

Plate 21   BANANA: PISANG MAS

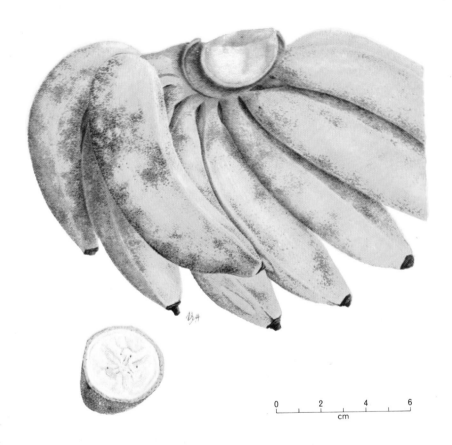

Plate 22 BANANA: PISANG RASTALI

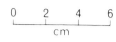

0   2   4   6
cm

Plate 23   BANANA: PISANG TANDUK

0   2   4   6
cm

Plate 24   COCONUT (*Cocos nucifera*)

many years it was thought that the parent banana originated in India, but more recent research points to the Malay Peninsula, though wild plants still grow throughout the tropics of the Old World (India, Asia, Africa). In Malaysia they are very common in the jungle especially in damp open places, but the fruits of these are usually very small, hard and full of seed. They are generally grouped under the names: *Pisang hutan, P. sorong* or *P. karuk,* and the ones eaten by the aborigines, *Tilai* which appears to be a generic name (also *Kukean* by the Semang tribe in Perak).

Thriving in Malaysia's moist, hot climate, the cultivated bananas are common in gardens and the crops are a feature of the countryside, yet the fruit are not exported, all being consumed locally. The banana plants have fibres in their leaves which are used as string by country people, and the Manila Hemp (*Abaca* or *Pisang Manila*) which produces the famous ropes and cords, comes from the fibres of a wild banana, *Musa textilis.* Centuries ago, before the introduction of manufactured cotton, banana fibres were probably used for making cloth in Malaysia. Generally speaking, however, the fibres of the cultivated fruiting plants are not strong.

A banana plant is just a giant herb, without any really hard tissues and no true stem. The leaves start about ground level, their bases closely overlapping and forming a sort of trunk. When a stem is cut across, these tightly packed leaf-bases can be seen, with the fruiting stem pushing through the middle. After a bunch of fruit has ripened, no more are produced and the stem is usually cut down. Hence the common saying : *Tiada akan pisang berbuah dua kali.**
Suckers develop around the base of the old plant and these produce the fruit of the new generation. Banana leaves are enormous when one considers that they start at ground level and a plant may be 15 feet tall. In most species the stalk carrying the flower is drooping, the groups of flowers being protected by bracts which later fall. The pointed tip to the flowerhead, covered with red or purple bracts, contains the male flowers (*kelepek jantung*) and these have a delicate flavour when cooked. The female flowers which develop into the fruits are further back, nearer the main stem. Fruits form in groups on the now thick stalk; each one of these is called a HAND, and an

---

*The banana does not bear twice. (Similar to "Once bitten, twice shy.")

individual fruit a FINGER. They vary greatly in size, shape and flavour, and there are dozens of different forms cultivated in Malaysia, each having many local names. In West Malaysia, the cultivated fruits may be divided into two main groups: BANANA for those eaten raw, and PLANTAIN which have to be cooked first, as the raw flavour is usually unpleasant or tasteless. In this, it has followed the West Indies, but unfortunately in India and Ceylon these two names are synonymous. Both are borrowed from the Portuguese who adapted the word "banana" from a West African one. In Malay, *Pisang* is the generic name for all kinds, the different forms or races being distinguished by adjectives, thus *Pisang mas,* the golden banana. The Plantain are conveniently grouped under *Pisang tanduk.* Some of the best known of the Malaysian forms are briefly described below.

BANANA: PISANG (*Musa paradisiaca*)
Under this heading come nearly all the best-known table bananas and most of these are commonly seen in the markets.

Plate 20

PISANG AMBON, P. embun, P. bunga, P. medji, Jamaican Banana, Gros Michel
Thai: Kluai-hom
> Fruit long, green at first then pale yellow; skin thick and easily peeled; flesh cream.

The plant grows to about 15 feet in height; the stems are usually mottled with very dark marks. There are 8 or 9 hands on a stem, each having 15–17 fingers. Fingers (fruits) are from 6½–8 inches long and about 1½ inches wide. This as the Gros Michel of the West Indies is exported to Europe in large quantities, and it is also grown commercially in the Canary Islands and other subtropical islands. *Pisang ambon* transports well and is the common banana served in hotels in this country.

Pisang hijau (*P. masak hijau*) which comes in this group, is sometimes sold as *P. ambon.* The skin is always flushed with green even when ripe; the fingers fall very easily from the hands and the flavour is sweet.

P. susu, which is less frequently seen, comes from a small plant no more than 9 feet in height. There are about 10 fingers to each hand; the skin and flesh are light yellow and the flavour very sweet. It is also one of the *ambon* group.

50

PISANG MAS, P. emas   Plate 21
Thai: Kluai-khai

> Fruit very short, golden yellow skin and flesh; skin adhering;
> blackish marks when ripe.

A dwarf plant with a yellow-green stem and small hands of fruit.
Fingers are about 3 × 1½ inches; the skin is thin and clings to the
flesh, which is a rich yellow colour. This is a popular banana and
is more expensive than the following form (*P. rastali*). It is occasionally served in hotels but does not carry well, bruising easily.

Pisang lilin which is a form of this, has a waxy bloom over the
skin, and the fruits are often sharply ridged. Popular, but not
commonly seen for sale.

PISANG RASTALI, P. tali   Plate 22
Thai: Kluai-nam-wa

> Fruit medium size, yellow with black spots; skin thin and
> easily peeled; flesh white or pale cream.

The plant grows to about 12 feet in height, with dark green stems
which have reddish-brown markings. The fruit bunch on a stem is
about 3½ feet long; there are 8–9 hands and about 12 fingers per
hand. Each finger is about 4–5 × 1¾ inches. The skin is of fine texture,
yellow with black spots eventually becoming dark all over. The thin
skin peels extremely easily, and the flesh is fine in texture; fruits
improve in flavour by being kept until quite mature. *Pisang rastali*
does not carry well, for it bruises rapidly and the fingers fall very
easily, tearing the skin.

This is one of the sweetest flavoured bananas in Malaysia, and
they are usually cheaper than the other well-known ones. There are
many forms and are very commonly seen in the markets. Some are
called *Pisang monyet*, the 'monkey banana', a disparaging name given
to those of little importance. The name *'rastali'* which appears to
have come from the Hindi, is apparently not identical with the banana
of the same name in south India.

There are very many more different kinds which will probably
be seen in various markets, and most noticeable would be the *Pisang
raja udang* (Thai: *Kluai-nak*). It has very large fruit with fingers
up to 10 inches or more long, dark reddish skin, and the flesh, inclined to be coarse has a pleasant flavour. *Pisang raja* is also large

and thick, but has a yellow skin. Neither appears to be commonly seen except perhaps on the East Coast, but the latter is commonly sold in Java.

PLANTAIN: PISANG TANDUK (*Musa paradisiaca* subspecies *sapientum*)

PISANG TANDUK, Plate 23
Thai: Kluai-kok
> Large sized fingers often about a foot a length. Skin usually green or greenish-yellow, with dark blotches appearing with maturity. The flesh is rather deep yellow.

Other well-known forms include: *Pisang abu* with a waxy bloom on the greenish skin; it is also called Ashy Plantain. *Pisang awak* (*awak betul, awak legor*) with blotchy skins which are yellow, and *awak legor* has many seeds. *Pisang talon,* is not so common and has yellow skin and soft pale flesh.

The bananas which are an important source of food to the people of Malaysia, are high in starch and when fully ripe, Vitamin A, sugars and phosphorus. Naturally there are many ways of preparing the fruit apart from eating it raw. *Pisang rimpi,* for instance are preserved strips of fruit dried in the sun, and will keep more or less indefinitely.

THE PALM FAMILY (*PALMAE*)

An enormous family ranging from the warm temperate climates to the tropics; it is well represented in Malaysia and the Pinang or Betel Palm (*Areca catechu*) is cultivated for its nuts which become the chewing Betel. The Date palm (*Phoenix dactylifera*) was cultivated by the ancient Egyptians and today is grown commercially in many of the arid tropical countries.

COCONUT: KELAPA (*Cocos nucifera*) Plate 24
Nyiur (mainly in Penang and the northern states),
Kelapa gading (dwarfs).
Thai: Ma-phrao   Tamil: Tennai
This is a well-known and familiar palm of the humid tropics, and

has been cultivated from remote times. No one knows exactly which is its country of origin. Naturalists and explorers have been debating this for centuries, for its dispersal was widespread even in ancient times, and there are many forms or races of the one species. The genus *Cocos,* has four species, three of these being native to America, the other being the Coconut. Fossil nuts of yet another species have been found in the north of New Zealand. The fruit of the Coconut is well adapted for travelling hundreds of miles by sea without the aid of man, and this suggests that it was originally coastal.

In Malaysia the trees may be divided into two main groups; the *dwarfs* and the *talls**. The dwarfs are commonly called King Coconuts and are short almost squat palms, not as common as the talls, nor do they tolerate such a wide range of soils. They do however, produce a very high yield, and because they are shorter, are easier to harvest. The talls are of course, the familiar Coconut palms we see everywhere in Singapore and Malaysia, with the long, often sloping trunks, and the tufts of waving, deep green leaves, and the smooth green fruits which appear to have no stalks.

Coconut trees are evergreen; old leaves falling off whilst new ones are being formed; the stem (trunk) does not increase its width with age as is the case with most of the other fruit trees. The trunk is ringed by scars from the fallen leaf bases. Flowers are in sprays from near the top of the palm, and the male and female are separate. Male flowers are on the spray-end, away from the trunk, but the female which are fewer in number are near the base of the spray, by the trunk. Trees bear fruit 4–6 years after planting the fruit (nut), and usually live about 50–60 years, producing fruit at frequent intervals in the good strains.

The nut consists of a smooth outer skin covering a wide fibrous layer; it is this layer that gives the fruit its bouyancy in water and enables it to float in the sea without harm. The centre is a bony covering pitted with 3 small marks where the covering is thin, this is provision for the shoot and the root of the young plant to emerge after germination. Inside is white flesh surrounding a hollow which is filled with liquid, which provides moisture for the new sprouting plant.

---

*descriptions from *The Coconut Palm,* see Ministry of Agriculture.

53

Fruits should be picked when unripe for, if left to fall, germination may have already commenced and then the flesh is past its best. Also they should be of medium size and nearly round, longer shapes usually have too much husk; there should be liquid inside and one hears this by shaking the fruit.

In nearly every way, Coconut is a most important and valuable plant to man, and lucky is the castaway who finds himself on an island on which the palm is growing. If he is intelligent he will discover he has water and food from the fruit, clothing, thatching and building materials from the leaves and trunk, utensils from the hard shell, even toddy if he is so inclined and knows how to make it.

In commerce, trees also provide coir matting from the husks, oil from the nuts, buttons from the hard shell, and the whole nut is exported to non-tropical countries. There are many uses in medicine; yeast can be obtained from the plant, toddy or *arak* is obtained by tapping near the top of the tree by the new growth. This is a drink which ferments rapidly, but before fermentation, is used for making palm sugar. Husks are used for fuel and from the white flesh *santan* is obtained. This is a necessity in most Malay and Muslim Indian curries; it is made by grating the moist flesh and squeezing it through a cloth. This comes out thick and creamy and a second amount is made with the addition of some water, then squeezing again; this is much thinner (called first and second santan). Both are used in curry and other spiced foods.

SELECT BIBLIOGRAPHY

AGRICULTURE, MINISTRY OF, Federation of Malaya publications:
'Malayan Food Composition Table' *Department of Ag. Scientific Series, 23.* 1949
'Home Canning & Jam Making' *Ministry of Ag. Bulletin, 35.* 1958
'The Pineapple in Malaya' *Ministry of Ag. Bulletin, 36.* 1959
'The Coconut Palm' *Ministry of Ag. Bulletin, 41.* 1959

BROWN, W.H. *Useful Plants of the Philippines.* 3 vols. Philipp. Natl. Museum. 1950

BURKILL, I.H. *A Dictionary of the Economic Products of the Malay Peninsula.* 2 vols. Ministry of Agriculture and Cooperatives, Kuala Lumpur. New edn. 1966

CHILD, R. *Coconuts.* Longman London 2nd Edn. 1974

COBLEY, L.S. *An Introduction to the Botany of Tropical Crops.* 1956

CORNER, E.J.H. *Wayside Trees of Malaya.* 2 vols. Govt. Printer, Singapore. 1954

GOUGH, K.A. *A Garden Book of Malaya.* 1940

GRIST, D.H. *An Outline of Malayan Agriculture.* Department of Agriculture, Federation of Malaya. 1950

HILL, A.F. *Economic Botany.* McGraw-Hill. 1952

HOLTTUM, R.E. *Plant Life in Malaya.* Longman Malaysia. 1954
Gardening in the Lowlands of Malaya. Straits Times Press, Singapore. 1953

MACMILLAN, H.F. *Tropical Planting and Gardening.* MacMillan, London. 1948

MOLESWORTH ALLEN, B. *Some Common Trees of Malaya.* Eastern Universities Press, Singapore. 1957

OCHSE, J.J. & BAKHUIZEN VAN DEN BRINK, R.C. *Fruit and Fruit Culture in the Dutch East Indies.* 1931

POPENOE, W. *Manual of Tropical & Sub-tropical Fruits.* 1924

PURSEGLOVE, J.W. *Tropical Crops, Dicotyledons (2 vols.), Monocotyledons (2 vols.)* Longman London. 1968 and 1972

RIDLEY, H.N. *Flora of the Malay Peninsula.* 5 Vols. L. Reeve & Co., London. 1922–25

SIMMONDS, N.W. *Bananas.* Longman London. 2nd Edn. 1966

SINGAPORE, Director of Botanic Gardens (Ed.) *The Garden's Bulletin.* A series from 1921. Singapore National Printers.

STONE, B.C. 'A New Wild Citrus species from Malaya' *The Planter* 48 : 90–92. 1972. Inc. Soc. of Planters, Kuala Lumpur.

STONE, B.C., LOWRY, J.B., SCORA, R.W., and JONG, K. 'Citrus halimii, a new species from Malaya and Peninsular Thailand' *Biotropica* 5(2) : 102–110 Soc. Trop. Biology.

STURROCK, D. *Fruits for Southern Florida.* 1959

VAN STEENIS, C.G.G.J. (Ed). *Flora Malesiana.* An Illustrated Systematic Account of the Malaysian Flora. Publ. under auspices of Kebun Raya Indonesia and Rijksherbarium, Leiden, Netherlands. Noordhoff-kolff N.V., Djakarta and Holland. Series I (vols. 1, 4, 5, 6); Series II (1). 1950

WATSON, J.G. 'Malayan Plant Names' *Malayan Forest Records, No.* 5 1928

WHITMORE, T.C. (Ed.) *Tree Flora of Malaya* 2 Vols. Longman Malaysia. 1972, 1973

GLOSSARY

ALTERNATE (for leaves): in two rows on the stem, but not opposite each other.

ANTHERS: The pollen-bearing part of the stamens.

CALYX: The outer part of a flower, and covering the petals in bud, comprising all the sepals.

COROLLA: Comprising all the petals.

DECIDUOUS: When all the leaves fall and leave the tree bare.

DICOTYLEDON: Plants producing two seed leaves (the first ones after germination).

EVERGREEN: Bearing leaves all the year round (see Deciduous).

FAMILY: A group of related plants of different *genera*.

FLOWER: Female: containing only *ovary* and *style,* no anthers. Male: containing the *stamens* only which hold the *anthers.* Unless otherwise stated in the text, a flower will contain both male and female organs.

FORM: A variation of a species which probably will not breed true (see Race).

FRUIT: The seeds and their container, whether fleshy or dry.

GENUS (plural Genera): The "surname" of related plants within a family.

HERB, HERBACEOUS: Plants which are not woody or very hard.

JOINED: Where a leaf or flower stalk joins the stem but does not break off easily.

JOINTED: As above, but where the join falls apart easily, and the joint can be seen.

LATEX: Milky juice.

LEAFLETS: When a leaf is divided into small leaf-like segments, usually small, along a communal stalk.

LEAFSTALK: This joins the leaf-blade to the branch; if missing, then the leaf is said to be *sessile.* See also under winged.

LEAVES: *Simple,* not divided into leaflets; *lobed,* divided but not to the central vein or midrib of the leaf. See also under margin.

MARGIN (of a leaf): *entire,* smooth edge, not *serrate* or *toothed.*

MONOCOTYLEDON: When the germinating seed produces one leaf.

OPPOSITE: Leaves arranged usually in pairs at the same level, on the stem.

OVARY: Part of the female flower which will later contain the seeds.

POLYMORPHIC: Having several forms.

RACE: A variation in a species, but which may breed true, from seed (see *Form*).

SEPALS: The individual outer parts of a flower, and collectively called a calyx.

SESSILE: See Leafstalk.

SERRATE:	A margin that is not smooth, but has saw-like teeth.
SPECIES (plural Species):	Individuals of a genus.
STAMENS:	The male part of the flower which hold the anthers.
STIGMA:	The part of the style which receives the pollen-grains from the anthers.
STIPULE:	A small appendage usually at the base of a leaf-stalk (in this book).
STYLE:	The female organ between the ovary and the stigma.
TEETH (toothed):	Minute marginal lobes.
TENDRIL:	Part of a leaf, leafstalk or stem adapted for climbing.
WINGED (of a leafstalk):	An appendage, narrow or wide, on either side of a leafstalk, and usually the same colour and texture as the leaf blade.

GLOSSARY OF MALAY WORDS

ABU ash
AIR water or liquid .
AMBON from Amboyna
ASAM (also Masam), acid or sour
AWAK you (familiar term); trunk of a body

BATU stone or rock
BELANDA Hollander; when used with fruit names, means different from the familiar fruit.
BESAR large
BESI iron
BETAWI Batavia
BETUL accurate or straight
BIJI seed or pip
BUAH fruit
BUAYA crocodile
BUBUR pulpy or sticky (in food)
BUNGA flower

CERMAI a tree with acid fruit
CUIT gesticulations with fingers

EMAS see Mas
EMBON see Ambon

GELUGUR fluted
GERAT ridging as on a fingernail
GETAH latex

HIJAU green and dark colours of the jungle and sea
HUTAN jungle or forest

JAMBU generic term for various fruits especially *Eugenia*
JANTAN male or masculine
JANTUNG heart or core
JERUK acid fruit; Javanese for *Citrus*

KARUK torch made of dried leaves
KELEPEK flip-flap (onomatopoeic)
KESTURI musk
KUCING cat

LAUT sea or ocean
LILIN wax or candle
LIMAU generic term for *Citrus* fruits

LOTONG leaf-eating monkey

MANIS sweet; also light in colour
MAS gold (has many meanings)
MASAM see Asam
MATA eye
MAWAR rose and rose water
MELAKA Malacca
MENILA Manila
MENTEGA butter
MENTIMUN see Timun
MERAH red
MONYET monkey

NIPIS thin

PANTUN verse, usually of great antiquity. Generally used to convey a specific message concealed in verse in the last two lines. The first two are usually for elegance, portraying something of beauty, particularly scenery.
PERSEGI see Segi
PISANG generic term for bananas
PUTIH white
PURUT rough skinned

RAJA King, prince (also Rajah)
RAMBUT hair of the head, hence Rambutan
RAYA mighty or great

SAMBAL condiments eaten with curry
SEGI corner or angle
SELASEH the herb Basil
SORONG pushing out
SUSU breast; the common word for milk

TANDUK horn, of the two-horned animals
TANJUNG cape or headland
TIMUN cucumber; gourd

UBI tuber of a plant; commonly potato
UDANG prawn; crayfish

INDEX

ENGLISH AND OTHER NAMES (THAI, TAMIL) *are in ordinary type*
MALAY NAMES *are in bold type*
LATIN NAMES *are in italic type*
FAMILIES *are in small capitals*
The sound formerly spelt 'ch' in Malay is now spelt 'c', e.g.
chempedak is now cempedak, chiku is now ciku, etc.

60